# Cell Level Meditation

## Breathing with The Wisdom & Intelligence of The Cell

Patricia Kay, MA and Barry Grundland, MD

SIMPLY WONDER, LLC

Printed and bound in The United States of America

Cover and book design: Heather Kibbey, Northwest Publishers Consortium
www.NPCBooks.com

ISBN: 978-0-615-27954-1

*The Guest House,* Rumi (translated by John Moyne and Coleman Barks), *Say I Am You,* Maypop, copyright ©1994, used with permission

"Chiyo-ni" from *Women in Praise of the Sacred: 43 Centuries of Spiritual Poetry by Women*, HarperPerennial, copyright ©1994, Jane Hirshfield, editor, used with permission

"Ono no Komachi" and "Izumi Shikibu" from *The Ink Dark Moon, Love Poems by Ono no Komachi and Isumi Shikibu, Women of the Ancient Court of Japan*, Vintage Books, copyright ©1986, Jane Hirshfield and Mariko Aratani, used with permission

*Selected quotations from Love Poems from God*, Penguin Books, copyright ©2002 Daniel Ladinsky and used with permission.

Selected quotations from *The Gift, Poems by Hafiz*, Penguin Books, copyright © 1999 Daniel Ladinsky and used with permission.

Brush painting by Sengai (reversed for the Western mind), Japan, c. 1830, Mitsu Art Gallery, Tokyo.

**Simply Wonder, LLC**

PO Box 12591

Olympia, WA 98508-2591

**website:** www.CellLevelMeditation.com

**email:** SimplyWonder@gmail.com

# Table of Contents

We dedicate this book—

to all who have done this work, as well as all who will.

# Foreword

Dr. Barry Grundland is a psychiatrist whose specialty area might be called psychoneuroimmunology. This is a big word that basically means mind-body healing. For over 40 years, he's been working with people as a true healer—one who helps others come to Wholeness, or to a sense of being who they really are. Barry has worked with people all over the world and helped them heal from things modern-day medicine hasn't been able to cure. He has also worked creatively with some of the most evolved people on the planet to develop their talents more fully. Of all his extraordinary accomplishments, he says he's most proud of his work and skills in child psychiatry.

It is Barry who named and developed the practice of Cell Level Meditation. He doesn't seem interested in writing, however. Once when I asked him about this, he replied that he didn't like to stop the flow of the Mystery. Somehow when we write about things, we define them, and Barry is more interested in experiencing the Mystery than defining it. He says,

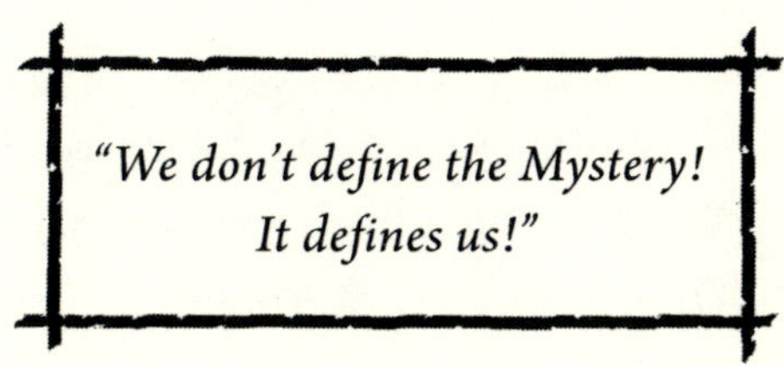

In writing the "qualifications" that give me the authority to write this book, I confess first of all, I didn't go to medical school. One time, Barry said, "Thank God they didn't get their hands on you," which made me feel better for awhile, but it is frankly something lacking in my development. Perhaps Life meant me to develop in a deeply feminine, more organic way, since my true passions were more mystical, while wanting to be in service within the healing arts.

After college and a decade in education, I moved to Mexico. My life shifted radically through childbirth. The experience was so powerful, we moved back to the US for several years, so I could go to midwifery school. Then we moved back to Mexico, where my doctor-husband, and I founded a People's Clinic. I spent the next decade learning about the life-force through birth and death (I had five near-death experiences during that time), and the study of homeopathy. The last decade brought me to live at the edge of a wetland, in the woods, to go deeper into silence and the patterns behind things, which opened my awareness to the Cell and the worlds within it.

They say the teacher comes when the student is ready. I must say I've been blessed with many wonderful and generous teachers in my life. When I asked Barry if I could study with him by listening in on the sessions he would have with my husband when he got cancer, he was thoughtful for while and seemed to be sensing into something. Finally, he said, "I'll work with you separately." And so it began. Perhaps in the pause, the gods intervened. It was a fateful moment.

From the alchemical alliance of our student/teacher relationship, in which the teacher and the student have been engaged in a living discourse over time, we bring you this book. By writing it, we are ever mindful of the dangers of losing the very essence of an important quality of working within the Mystery: It is most alive when there is a dialogue going on, when relationship is being forged in the gap between the known and the unknowable.

We have written the book in a conversational tone, asking you to listen into the reaches of your own thoughts, experiences and intuition. We do recognize the one-sidedness of this, and persist in the writing because we want to offer you a practical tool that opens doors of wonder and beauty that you can discover in dialogue with yourself and the self you'll find in every cell. This tool, which we hope you will make your own, has healing power, and being healers, how can we resist the urge to write it down? We do hope this book points you toward the Mystery...without defining it!

Patricia Kay
February, 2009

# Preface

Harmony Hill is a retreat center, nestled on a hillside facing the Hood Canal and the majesty of the Olympic Mountains, in Washington State. People come here to find inspiration, support, camaraderie, nourishment for the body and soul, as well as tools for helping to heal themselves of cancer. I learned of Barry Grundland's work through my friend, Barbara Riefle, a successful business woman from New York. Barbara attended one of our cancer retreats shortly after surgery disclosed she had a rare cancer of the appendix. Her diagnosis was a real shock to her and was compounded by the fact that there was no known medical treatment. After the retreat, Barbara set about finding every resource she could that would give her quality time for the remainder of her life. Through her yoga instructor in New York City, Barbara was introduced to Barry, and she soon became his student and immersed herself in learning some of his meditation techniques. She even visited at the home of Barry and his wife, Adrianne, in California, for one week so she could focus completely on this new healing technique.

Barry recognized Barbara's deep hunger for finding inner calm, and when she returned to New York, he arranged to meditate with her every day by phone. She looked forward to her time with him and made sure the hour she set aside for this was uninterrupted. I was impressed by the changes that I could see cell meditation was having on her. Years later, when I received a diagnosis of cancer, Barbara encouraged me to work with him. Although I had a previous meditation practice, Barry's support enhanced and deepened my meditations considerably. Immersing into my own cells with the breath was a wonderful new experience. I know his help was a significant component of my healing.

A few years later, Barry came to Harmony Hill as a teacher in residence for a month, and I saw how he worked with over 30 people, in a non-intrusive, supportive way. He was tireless, and we could barely keep up with him! Barry is an extraordinary man. His enthusiasm for all of life is infectious! He can find amusement in the children's cartoon, "Sponge Bob," and shift in a heartbeat to an informed appreciation of the great philosophers. He keeps abreast of modern medicine, world events, loves baseball, revels in his grandchildren, consults corporate leaders, takes a homeless person to lunch and finds new ways to make complex systems more effective. One of the stories that moved me was learning that he had mandated that doors be placed on the bathroom stalls when he served as Psychiatrist for the Army. He wanted the men to have one place where they could have some privacy and at least take a few minutes for some calming breaths.

Barry has a tremendous love for nature. He incorporates much gratitude for the earth's beauty into his teachings. He helped me learn to imagine bringing the life-force of the trees, ferns, and flowers (anything alive and growing), into my cells as part of healing. To this day (many years later), I can hear his joyful voice when I meditate outside, surrounded by nature's glory.

Patricia has given voice to the work in a simple, but deep way. This book is nourishing to read and soothing. If you read each chapter slowly and savor it, practice it and breathe with it, you'll receive a gift. Then, if you go back for a second and third reading, you'll begin to find places in yourself you may not have noticed, and when you listen to them and breathe with them, you will move in the direction of greater harmony and balance in yourself. Part of our mission at Harmony Hill is to help people find healing inside themselves. This book helps do just that.

Gretchen Schodde, ARNP, MN
Executive Director, Harmony Hill
Union, WA

# Introduction

***May all things move and be moved in me***
***and know and be known in me.***
***May all creation***
***dance for joy within me.***

Chinook Psalter
Quoted in: A Grateful Heart

Cell Level Meditation is a vehicle for finding our way "home." We take the breath to our cells, offering them our deepest desire to be happy and healthy and strong. In some way, they hear us and respond. (Or maybe we hear them asking for the breath!) This meditative form is a gift that helps the mind and the body come into a healing relationship, which in turn, helps us be ourselves in fullness.

In the *Odyssey*, the great mythological journey told by Homer, the hero, Odysseus, spends years trying to get home. To get there, he goes through all kinds of trials and tribulations. He has to use every kind of skill and every clever device you can imagine. He always has to have his wits about him because something new and different is always coming up, and he has to have the courage of his creative response for each ordeal. Of course, this is the archetypal human journey we all are on in one form or another. We are trying to find out who we are and how to be full in that. I would describe this as health: ***being fully who we are and having the body, mind and spirit in full congruence as an expression of that.*** As you begin taking this journey for yourself, you'll discover that the journey into the body, into the cells is quite an adventure! You can take it for your own creative reasons. This little book is a road map for the journey inside.

Several years ago, during a particularly difficult period in my life, I went to the beach in Mexico with some friends for renewal, healing and inspiration. One day, I was out swimming in the ocean, and as I was coming in, I got taken by a wave and slammed against some rocks. It wasn't too serious, but my foot was scraped and bleeding. And I was jarred by the experience of being taken by the powerful force of the ocean.

I stumbled out of the ocean with my scraped and bleeding foot. I was a little dazed, but I managed to walk down the beach where I sat under a huge rock. In the shade provided there, I intuitively went into deep meditation, experiencing fully the sensation in my foot without "doing" anything but noticing it and being present with the sensations.

Within seconds, an image came to me. In my mind's eye, I was seeing a moving kaleidoscope of orange shapes, like petals on a flower; the color was very brilliant. I was entranced by this spontaneous vision that came to me. I felt calmed by it. After a while in this meditative experience I began to "see" long, slender "fingers," purplish in color, coming together. I felt some excitement, and wondered if I were seeing *Arnica* flowers, since I'd never seen them. I am a homeopath, and certainly this is the remedy I would have taken if I'd had it with me, since *Arnica* is a plant used herbally and homeopathically to heal the trauma of bruised and injured tissue. I wondered if I were connecting with it, receiving its healing properties. By now, my foot no longer hurt, and I realized I had been healed. I opened my eyes and looked at my foot. The skin, which had been broken, was totally healed. There was only some minor swelling of the area.

As you can imagine, I was amazed by this very dramatic healing. I felt touched by something very holy. I closed my eyes and went into this sense of amazement I was feeling. A question came to me: Did I want the power to heal people? I pondered this question and followed it down a path of self-inquiry. I discovered through this that I didn't want this power. Somehow it wasn't interesting to me to have such a power, but what did (and does) interest me was accompanying people in their own discoveries of healing and unfolding and giving them any tools that might help them.

I came out of my reverie and walked back down the beach to where my friends were. Now, one of the people I was with was my dear friend and mentor in homeopathy, Rosa. I asked Rosa what color Arnica flowers were, and she said, "They're orange." Then I wondered if I had connected with their essence in the first image given to me: the kaleidoscope of orange shapes. Because of the way my mind works, I believe I somehow captured what I call the "geometry" behind the form. And, I understood that the purplish "fingers" I'd seen were cells reuniting.

This was one of my more dramatic moments with Cell Level Meditation. It was about 7 or 8 months later that a friend told us to contact Barry, and I began to work with him. Over the years of working with him, listening to him and accompanying other people in their healing journeys, I have been blessed and delighted to travel into myself and others, to the cellular level and beyond. I have witnessed the ordinary power of the extraordinary bodies we live in as they (and we) come into healing, and I just love that!

Each cell is kind of a mini-world that contains the whole in a peculiar way. At the most basic of levels, each cell does all the things a whole body does: it breathes, it has intelligence, it takes in food and converts it to energy for creating new things, it cleanses itself, it renews itself and communicates with other cells. I also discovered that each cell seems to have memories of events, beliefs, opinions, preferences and habits. And there is color and movement, activity and rest, sounds and rhythm.

I have also discovered that the inner journey inspires a similar kind of wonder and reverence as the outer journey. The journey in or the journey out—they're surprisingly similar and they seem to mirror each other. Looking out at the night sky inspires awe and reverence.

We look up into the inky dark sky that holds glittery lights and feel a deep sense of wonder. Going into the body—the tissues, the organs, the cells, the molecules and beyond—is similarly, breathtaking. The words spoken by the ancient master, Hermes Trismegistus ring true:

***"As above, so below.***
***As within, so without."***

Yes! Wonder and reverence above and reverence and wonder below.

It's true, I was probably primed for the experience I described above. I began wondering about mystical things when I was very young. I learned to meditate just out of college. When I was in midwifery school in the 80's, I learned about the power of guided visualization, through the work of Lewis Mehl-Madrona, Carl and Stephanie Simonton and Milton Erikson. In fact, I used guided visualization many times during my 12-year tenure as a midwife, sometimes with amazing results, and sometimes with disappointment. I had my doubts about it.

Being honest with doubt, looking it in the eye, acknowledging it's there and sometimes turning my back on it, helps me go to a deeper listening. Again and again, I am brought to a very humbling reality: healing is a mysterious journey. I don't control it. I don't get to decide who heals and who doesn't. I have a tendency to want to know the answers, to know how to do things, but again and again, this journey is about letting go into the moment with all my best instincts and letting the Mystery direct the unfolding. It is much more beautiful and thorough than I am, and in fact, it's in the Mystery that healing happens.

# 1

# The Power of Meditation—The Rationale

***"It is the mark of an educated mind to be able to entertain a thought without accepting it."***

Aristotle
philosopher, 384-322 BC

Thanks to modern-day science, we've discovered that meditation is a key factor in any healing program. Dr. Dean Ornish includes it in his program for cardiac patients. And, of course, Dr. O. Carl Simonton brought the experience of guided visual imagery to help people with cancer to heal back in the 70's. Also, Dr. Bernie Siegel, along with many other medical doctors, has shown the results of using guided imagery to bring healing to the body. Dr. Mitchell Gaynor, an oncologist, teaches his patients to do a meditative kind of chanting, which has been very healing for many of them.

Joan Borysenko, PhD, clinical psychologist, co-founded and directed the Mind/body Clinical Programs at the Beth Israel Deaconess Medical Center, Harvard Medical School. She is one of the leading experts on stress, spirituality and the mind/body connection in a universe which she says is "fundamentally mysterious." Jon Kabat-Zinn, a professor at the University of Massachusetts Medical School, is well known for his work in mind-body medicine. He's found that patients trained in meditation have stronger immune systems than those who don't. And according to Ken Wilber, meditation training is the best way to accelerate the evolution of consciousness. The Institute of Noetic Sciences (IONS) is doing exciting research to bring Science and Spirit together, helping us to come to greater levels of understanding and healing and the reality of the mind-body connection.

In our culture, science is widely accepted as having the final say about what is "real." I get excited when western science validates what has been described as a mystical experience by great thinkers through the ages. I really get excited when a structure I've "seen" in meditation within an organ or cell is revealed by a new imaging technology. Our culture believes in science, and it's important to us to have credible people doing well-designed studies to show us that we are doing something "real," not just being superstitious or indulging in wishful thinking. To help your scientific mind, I've listed a few resources at the end of this book so you can have a satisfying mind-experience of work that's been done to show that the mind-body connection is "real," and that meditation is effective. Each of these resources, in turn, directs you to many more resources. There is so much available these days to give you information and inspiration. All of these studies and books serve as compasses that point the way until you've had your own unshakeable experiences.

However, it's the perennial wisdom of great spiritual traditions that has survived the test of time, while the "science" of every age up to now has been challenged, refined and changed as our level of awareness and understanding evolves. Maybe this just goes to show that our knowledge of the physical isn't as "solid" as we might think. In fact, it may point to the notion that the very "solidness" of the physical world isn't as "real" or unchanging as we tend to think. However, since recorded history, we have records of people pointing toward certain truths and spiritual principles that seem to hold up over time. These truths have a poetry about them. They quicken us when we hear or read them. They inspire us to our best selves. And they tend to show up in every tradition. The notion of treating others as we would like to be treated, known as the Golden Rule, for example, shows up in Christianity, Buddhism, Hinduism, Islam, and Judaism, just to name a few prominent spiritual traditions. And if you think about, and feel toward it, your body will sense the truth, the timeless truth of this statement, which we know as "Do unto others as you would have them do unto you." It just feels right, no?

Yet, there has been a long-standing tension between Science and Spirit. David Ray Griffin, a modern philosopher and theologian summarizes the dilemma: "Whereas scientific beliefs are based primarily on sensory perceptions, religious beliefs are based primarily on non-sensory perceptions." The great religious leaders and great scientists have been trying to reconcile these differences for a long time.

Within this form of meditation, we may be evolving our capacity to deepen and expand our sensory perceptions, thus bringing science and spirit together in a fluid, interactive dance of greater understanding and greater reverence for the magnificent structures we live in: our bodies! Clear down at the level of the cells, we are healing the split, allowing each perspective its due, attending to our senses (and extending them!) as well as staying open and in wonderment of things we don't know.

In our times, we are seeing a movement toward a respectful relationship between science and spirit. Some of the research showing the connection between the mind and the inner or subjective self, and the body and the outer or objective self is very exciting (and comforting to folks whose intuition has been tuned this way). I must say, however, that while the studies help us and open us to exploration, they can also lure us into thinking that somehow we can control what is deeply mysterious. I can hear Barry's words echo,

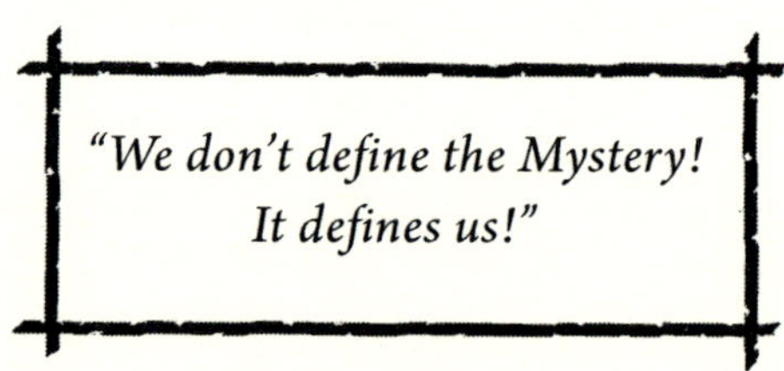

# 2

# Cell Level Meditation—In A Nutshell

***"I wonder why. I wonder why.***
***I wonder why I wonder.***
***I wonder why I wonder why***
***I wonder why I wonder."***

Richard P. Feynman,
physicist, 1918-1988

Let's begin to experiment with meditation. I am directing you toward three territories or places from which you can observe and participate.

## ● 1. The Silent Spaciousness

Notice the white part of this page…not the little black squiggles (the letters and words), but the white space.

This is no-thing-ness.

This is the background or the spaciousness the words are resting on. Notice what happens in your body when you just look at the white part of the page.

What do you notice?

Now, let's do something similar with the no-thing-ness all around you. There is airy space all around you. There is an air-filled space between you and the ceiling. Right? Close your eyes and notice this space around you. Notice that there is spaciousness all around you. Take 30 seconds to do this.

What do you notice?

Perhaps you noticed that there is simply nothing there. Yes! That's right. There's nothing!

No-thing! How strange, no? Here we are noticing that there is no-thing-ness all around us. There's just empty space.

There is a place always around us in every moment where there is no-thing; where things aren't configured yet, where all possibilities lie.

There is silence. Just notice **that** there is silence, spaciousness, emptiness, no-thing-ness.

By noticing this silence, just turning our attention toward it, we begin to open ourselves to new possibilities we hadn't thought to dream of.

We make a little space to go beyond our programming. As you travel along this journey of cell level meditation, you will certainly be surprised again and again about how deep this programming is. Some of the programming is really great. Some of it is...well, less than really great. However, in the field of no-thing-ness, we can open up to things we didn't know to dream of, possibilities we never imagined. Oooh! The Mystery.

## ■ 2. The Body

Very good! You have just had a very important experience in noticing silence and emptiness, no-thing. And that you can notice it whenever you want.

Let's move on to the next step.

Turn your awareness inward, to your body. Notice your body. There is definitely some-thing there, no? It's a real thing vs. the no-thing we were just noticing. There are many ways to approach the body. You can notice the whole body as one thing, part by part, tissues, organs and yes...cells.

One way to get started is to take a little trip through your body. So, I invite you to do this now so you begin to cultivate some experience of your own. Starting with your head, let's explore the qualities of the body. See what sensations you can actually notice. Let your curiosity out and use all your senses to see what you actually notice. We'll go through each body part.

Beginning with the head: tune in, and see what sensations you can be aware of in your head. Try to find a few words to describe anything you can notice (warmth, tingling, buzzing, heaviness, throbbing, and so on).

Move on down to your throat and neck. What can you detect there? (tightness, openness, tension, green, purple, minty, bubbly, creaky ,fluid...). Use all your senses.

Keep going down to your right arm—what do you notice?

Now, notice your left arm. Name the sensations you can detect there. You say nothing? How do you know it's there?

Keep noticing.

Now, turn your awareness to your shoulders. What can you feel or sense there? Is there warmth, heat, pulsation, tightness, lead weight?

Keep going—what can you notice about your chest? Pay attention. What can you actually feel, sense or perceive in some way? Maybe you are getting more relaxed and a vision will come to your mind's eye. It actually comes to you and you can notice it, so if that happens, it's there.

Move down to the abdomen. What's going on there? Use your curiosity to see what you can actually notice and name (gurgling, rushing, green slime, hollow, a taste arising in your mouth, an odor).

The back? Notice vertebrae by vertebrae. See what sensations you can detect.

Go to your lower back, butt, hips and pelvis. What's going on there?

Now let's go down the left leg, all the way down to the knee, to the calf, to the ankle, to the foot. Get curious and see if you can be a good observer of what you can actually be aware of.

You're getting it: now go down the right leg: thigh, notice; knee, notice; calf, notice; ankle, notice; foot, notice.

If my calculations are right, we've made it through the whole body, just noticing the sensations in each part. Do a quick body scan now, and see if you can notice anything about the whole. Stop a minute and describe in words what you notice.

If you are like a lot of people I know, you may be surprised to discover how much you could notice just by turning your attention to your body sensations. It's surprising how much is there, even on first glance, when you begin to pay attention. Remember my foot healing? This was all I did: notice. The foot healed itself.

## ▲ 3. The Breath

Ok, you now have an experience with no-thing and some-thing. Let's add one more thing:

The breath!

You are probably already breathing. Right? Now, I invite you to become aware of your breath:

***Here I am***
***Breathing.***
***I breathe in.***
***I breathe out.***

*Here I am:*
*Breathing in, Breathing out.*
*I feel the air coming into my nose.*
*I feel the air going out of my nose.*
*I feel the air coming in,*
*I notice the pause between breaths,*
*I feel the air going out,*
*I notice the pause.*
*I notice that without any thought at all,*
*The breath comes in, comes toward me.*
*From the silence, the breath comes toward me.*
*I do nothing to cause this to happen.*
*The breath comes in, on its own.*
*I feel wonder.*
*As I breathe out, I breathe into the wonder.*
*I breathe toward this sense of wonder.*
*I become this sense of wonder.*
*Wonder and I are the same thing!*

But I get ahead of myself. Please take a little break, and watch your breath. See what happens. What do you notice about paying attention to your breathing? Put this into a simple statement for yourself.

Let's go another step now. (You are moving along very quickly!)

You have noticed the spaciousness around yourself and no-thing, yes?

You have noticed there are many sensations going on in your body. Maybe you noticed these sensations shifted a little just because you were noticing them. But, you have noticed some-thing.

You have noticed that you breathe in from the empty space around you. There is breathing going on.

Now, I suggest that you notice that you are breathing in from the space around you. For the first time, we are going to do something: direct the breath. When you breathe out, try taking the breath into the sensations in your body. Pick one sensation that you can notice, and imagine that you are riding the breath into the body, into the sensation. Fully breathe into the sensation. Notice.

Go into the sensation with the breath, pouring the breath in. Notice.

Take breath from the spaciousness, breathe it into the sensation. Go into the sensation. Become the sensation. Keep breathing. Notice the sensation of the sensation. Become that. Keep breathing...

What happened?

# The Ingredients of Cell Level Meditation

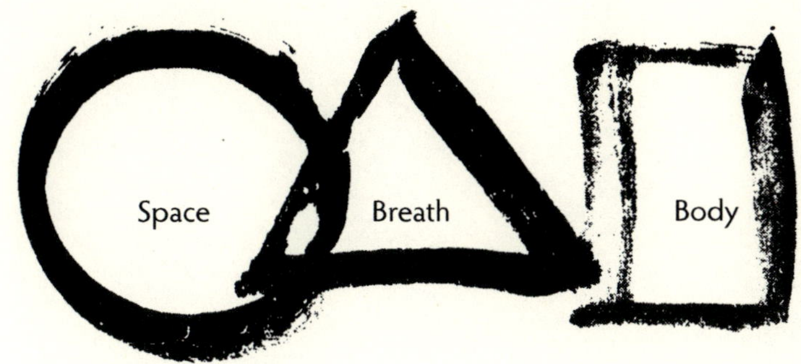


-Brush painting by Sengai, ca 1830,
in the Mitsu Art Gallery in Tokyo

There you have it: the ingredients of Cell Level Meditation.

- ● Your awareness of the spaciousness around you.
- ■ Your awareness of the body and any sensations you have there.
- ▲ From the spaciousness, breathe into your body, into the sensations you actually discover and become or merge with these sensations. (Keep going: notice the next sensation, breathing into it and becoming it...)

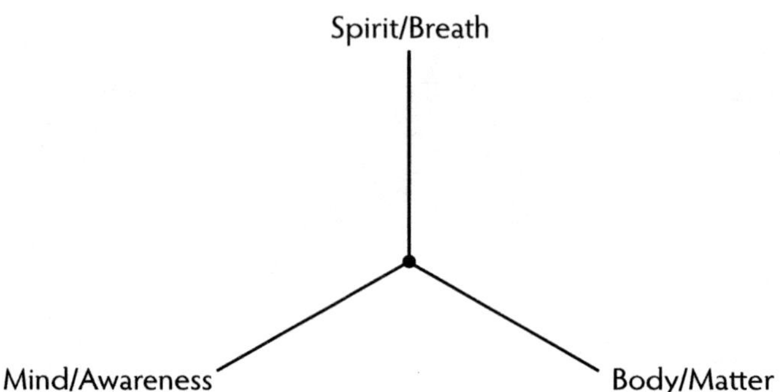


## To Summarize

You might say that the one who is doing the noticing is "the mind" or awareness. The breath might be called "the spirit," and the body, is, well…the body! By paying attention, you bring these three aspects of yourself together.

In the next three chapters, I'll explore each component of this triad a little more.

# 3
# The Mind

***From the mind***
***Of a single, long vine,***
***One hundred opening lives.***

Chiyō-ni
Haiku poetess, 1703-1775
translated by Jane Hirshfield

Your mind notices things. It thinks thoughts. That's what it's good at. That's its nature. (It can also drive you nuts when it won't shut-up.) So you have to engage your mind and let it do what it's good at. It loves having a job! So, you can ask it to come up with answers to such questions as:

"***Why am I doing this meditation?***"
Or "***Where shall I direct the breath?***"

It just loves being helpful.

You can use your mind to understand a basic principle of creation: you energize what you put your awareness on. Spiritual teachers talk about this principle. In fact there is a cute little rhyme that sums up this idea: "Energy flows where attention goes." And, you'll soon discover what they're talking about if you're paying attention.

Now, if you shine a flashlight on an object in the dark, that's where your attention goes, no? Given that this is so, what are you putting your energy on? Why are you doing a certain meditation? The answer to this is a touchstone that keeps you focused. If your intention is to heal from a certain illness, use that, perhaps loosely, but use it to guide the meditation. This is one job of the mind: to discover the intention and frame it into a statement that will help you have a focus.

It is pretty easy to get lost in reverie or to get sidetracked when you first sit down to meditate, especially if you have a lot on your mind. It's really common for the mind to wander off. It's just such a curious rascal! Gently, bring it back to the task at hand, touching base with your intention or noticing.

You can also reassure your mind that it can make a list of groceries to buy later. Over time, you may be interested in where your mind goes. Take your breath to that! The wandering off part—breathe to that. What does it feel like when your mind drifts away? What's happening in the body? Breathe into that.

There are so many possibilities for healing. But I do want to state that it can be very useful to have a clear intention which grounds the meditation and makes it more powerful. If you get lost, your mind has a job—to remember the intention, so you can go back to the breath, and pick up the thread, rather than wandering around aimlessly without focus.

To find your intention, simply get quiet and turn to the spacious silence. Breathe. Ask the question: ***Why am I doing this meditation?*** Breathe and see what comes to you. When the intention comes to you, check it out with your body. Your body doesn't know how to lie, and so when you state an intention for doing any given cell meditation, your whole body (and the whole collection of cells that make it up) will say "yes." You'll feel it. In fact, maybe it's the body that sent your mind the intention! ***Where did the thought/intention come from?*** When mind and body are in congruence, there is a sense that feels right. You feel at ease. How interesting that when there isn't congruence you experience the opposite: dis-ease.

In stating your intention, there is greater power in stating what you do want, instead of what you don't want. "I don't want this illness," is true, and it's more powerful to connect with "I do want to be healthy." When you think this thought, you can check into your body (do a little scan from head to toe) to see if there is a sensation calling to you. Notice that. Notice the body's call. Breathe into it, and your journey begins. As you breathe into your intention, the stage is set for the Great Intelligence to take you on the healing path of a given meditation.

Listen inside yourself to find your intention. You will feel quickened or more alive when you state what is really true for you.

You just can't fool the body. When you find your true intention, your body will relax, and you'll have the sense, "*That's it!*" This helps you get started.

Your true intention may be:

- ***I'm doing Cell Level Meditation because I'm healing my body from [you name the disease].***
- ***Or, I'm doing Cell Level Meditation because I am slimming my body to a more healthful weight.***
- ***Or, I'm doing Cell Level Meditation because I am training my muscles to swim faster.***

I've noticed that by taking the time to let my true intention come into focus, I've already begun to tune toward what is most helpful for healing. (A tip for those who sense the power of this, you can do this when you are working out or eating: align your intention, breath and body until it feels true to you, and you can enhance your workout or your digestion or your enjoyment of life.)

When your intention has come to you out of the Silent Spaciousness, begin to breathe. Notice your breathing. Then take the breath into your body. Let your body guide the way by letting sensations, images or sounds that you can actually perceive, guide you. Stay alert! Stay present to all the sensations that you may have. By taking the breath to the body again and again, your state of consciousness may change. Your brainwaves will probably be shifting frequencies into deeper states of awareness.

The frequency at which you need to be aware to find the cells begins to happen. You may have a heightened sense of awareness. You may notice a kind of liveliness that you hadn't really seen before—a liveliness that's always there and strangely familiar. Become receptive and see what comes toward you.

There are many ways this may happen for you. Some people are very visual and they tend to "see" things in their "mind's eye." Other people "hear" things. Others have a kind of epiphany and suddenly, they just know things, and it's hard to describe how they know them.

Stay loose with your experience. Just take the breath to whatever comes toward you. Use the breath to travel into the sensations. Become the sensations.

What's happening at the cell level is already happening. Go into it. Take the breath to the cells, however they show up. You may feel a tingling somewhere in your body—breathe to that. If you are working on your liver, breathe to it, become it and breathe some more. If a color shows up in your mind's eye, breathe to it, become it and breathe some more. Keep going.

It's pretty common to begin a meditation with a specific intention only to discover something very hidden that you never expected. By following the trail of going into what comes toward you, you can liberate energy, open doors, and find your way through to a deeper healing than you even thought was possible.

Oh! But who was it that put the bug in your ear to want to heal to begin with? Where did that come from?

# 4
# The Body

***"The great wisdom dwells in the body.
Fully away from all thoughts, it dwells in the body,
but is not produced in the body."***

A Sambhuti (Buddhist) Text

I must say, the human body is quite a wonder. It is a brilliant organism, made up of living cells. The cells are actually alive and responsive. They are the smallest living units. They are quite amazing.

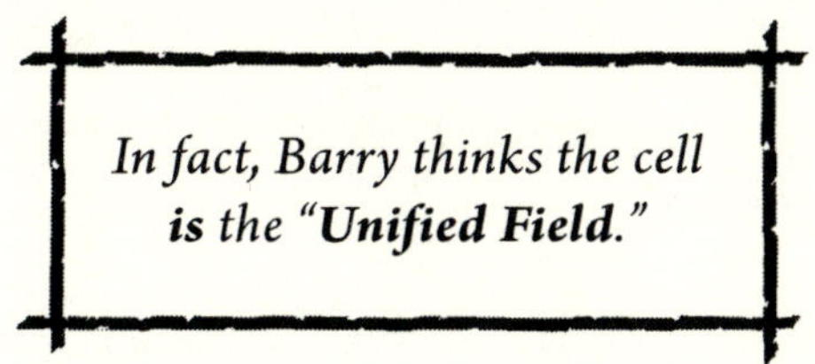


And they get together, in communities, and make up tissues and organs. These get together and give rise to the whole body. Trillions of cells get together, get along, and orchestrate life through the body.

The capacity of the body to stay healthy most of the time and to bring about its own healing from all kinds of disorders is quite amazing. Sometimes, it becomes even more intelligent by getting well from an illness as if something comes to greater awareness or a higher level of functioning as a result.

***"... I may have been beaten down by cancer, but I did rise—taller, stronger, more vibrantly alive than before."***

-RuthAnn McCann,
alumna of a cancer retreat at Harmony Hill in Union, Washington

Another woman echoes these words:

***"A part of me died. It had to happen, so something new could be born. I never thought I'd say this, but I am actually grateful for the cancer. I never would have come this alive had I not come through this journey. Now, I'm in partnership with all these different dimensions of me."***

-Debbie Hansen

What startling statements! Actually, it is not uncommon to hear statements like these from people who have healed from terrible diseases. By engaging the body consciously, you can discover all kinds of things about yourself.

And, after having sung its praises, I will also state that the body is quite a taskmaster! When it's out of order, you're miserable! Now this body of ours, as you probably know, is made up of basic building blocks—cells. Each cell is a little world that is quite lively.

Surrounding each cell is an outer covering, the cell membrane, which has a great intelligence about what is allowed in and out of the cell. This membrane has channels in and out of the cell, receptor sites that allow it to receive messages from other parts of the body. It makes decisions about who gets in and who stays out.

Inside of the cells all the functions are going on that keep the whole body alive: breathing, drinking, eating, eliminating, energy consumption and production, reproduction, and communication, and creation. And, you may be surprised to learn that the cell is responsive—it seems to enjoy attention. In fact, it seems to enjoy the same things you do!

Candace Pert, Ph.D., is a research professor in the Dept. of Physiology and Biophysics at Georgetown University Medical Center in Washington, D.C. Her descriptions of the biological capacities of cells are striking. She has discovered that there is dynamism involved between thoughts and cell responsiveness. The "stuff" of our bodies is not just inert and inanimate, but rather it is constantly shifting, changing, responding to conscious and unconscious signals. She has also noticed that the body actually responds to what we think, and we probably are responding to what it thinks as well.

***"Emotions and bodily sensations are intricately intertwined***
***in a bi-directional network in which each can alter the other.***
***Usually this process takes place at an unconscious level,***
***but it can also surface into consciousness***
***under certain conditions,***
***or be brought into consciousness by intention."***

Furthermore,

***"There are almost infinite pathways for the conscious mind to access—and modify—the unconscious mind and the body."***

This is a powerful statement—almost infinite pathways!

***Practically unlimited possibilities!***

The actual physical structures that are created in the cell as the dialogue between mind and body is going on is an exciting area of discovery, showing us that our thoughts are literally creative of such things as new polypeptides, hormones, new neural pathways and things way beyond the scope of this book.

When you start to explore this vast intelligence of matter itself, as it lives in your physical body, you will discover yourself, again and again. The imprint of who you are is in every cell.

As Jon Kabat-Zinn might say, "***Wherever I go, there I am.***"

# 5
# The Spirit

***The sky gave me its heart***
***Because it knew mine was not large enough to care***
***For the earth the way it did.***

Rabia of Basra
Muslim Sufi Saint , 717-801 AD,
translated by Daniel Ladinsky

The breath, the simple act of breathing, is the cornerstone of many types of meditation.

In many languages the word for breath and spirit are the same. You might contemplate the breath and the act of taking air in, the sensations you experience as you do this:

- the fact that you do it without thinking about it
- the fact that the air is always there for you
- the fact that it's free and it's freeing

There is something quite uplifting, expansive and wonder-evoking just in the simple act of breathing. And the breath is associated with the spirit.

Each time you breathe, you are participating in the Mystery! And when you do this with some awareness, you may have an experience of awe and wonder. The Vastness of the Infinite comes into the finite body. We take in the breath and merge with it, follow it, and in meditation, we play with it and pray with it!

In different spiritual traditions, there are specific breathing techniques that are used to evoke certain experiences. Some of these are quite elaborate and can be very powerful. As you might have guessed, the only specific instructions Barry and I have come up with to guide you into your body are to be aware THAT you're breathing and to take the spaciousness of the breath into your body. There, breath and body find relationship--the one with the other. And you? You are there as witness, amazed that you are there for something much more wonderful, inspiring and beautiful than you might have conjured up on your own.

And for our purposes, and this is very important, the Breath opens the channels of healing. The Breath takes us beyond the thinking of the small mind (that ***it*** is in charge of healing). The Breath opens the body and the mind to ***infinite possibilities***.

It takes us into no-thing-ness, beyond our conditioning, our programming and our habits, to possibilities not yet dreamed of. It stops us from "thinking" we are doing the healing and opens us to The Great Healing. What a relief!

*Breath!*
*Great Spirit!*
*Here I am!*
*Breath into the body.*
*Breath into the sensation in the body.*
*Breath into the color, the sound, the smell.*
*Breath into the flavor, the feel, the warmth.*
*Breath into the shape, the movement, the rhythm.*
*Breath into the very cells of this human body.*
*Here I am!*
*Already Whole*
*Here I am.*

# 6

# Not Knowing & Knowing Too Much

***"A hidden connection is stronger than an apparent one."***

Heraclitus
philosopher, 535-475 BC

We only have fragments from this Greek philosopher, but this statement is one of those perennial truths that's been on record since around 500 BC.

When you begin to meditate, you don't know what will come toward you. You don't have to know. In fact, it's probably what you don't know that has the greatest power and holds the greatest potential for your true healing. Remember the analogy of shining the flashlight in the dark room? Your intention shines that flashlight, but what steps into the beam of light, coming out of the darkness is often quite a big surprise.

As I describe Cell Level Meditation to you, I remind you and myself over and over,

***Life is really mysterious!***

Being able to stay open to that is such a gift, such a liberating gift. Don't worry, though, your mind will probably pop up over and over, trying to take charge, asking things like, "Why?" One student who worked with me came up with a great line to help herself when she noticed this happening: "Uh, oh! The 'whys' got me again." And then she'd go back to the silence, the experience of the body and the breath. And, you can help your mind stay curious by helping it ask better questions, like "Where is that going on in the body?"

Sometimes you think you're going to heal something. You begin to breathe and the breath takes you down a totally unexpected trail, opening doors, liberating cramped and musty ideas for a deeper healing in body and mind than you ever thought possible. Or, continuing with the flashlight analogy, monsters, vampires and 3-year-olds with sad faces step into the spotlight. You just never know what's going to show up. This can be a little scary!

In a poem by Hafiz, a Sufi poet, who lived from 1320 to 1389 (interpreted by Daniel Ladinsky in *The Gift*), he helps us realize we're not alone in our concern. It's somehow deeply human to recognize our place within the vast Mystery.

***A seed***
***Has sprouted beneath a gold leaf***
***In a dark forest.***

***This seed is seriously contemplating,***
***Seriously wondering about***
***The moseying habits***
***Of the Elephant.***

***Why?***

***Because***
***In this lucid, wine-drenched tale***
***The Elephant is really--***
***God,***

***Who has His big foot upon us,***
***Upon the golden leaf under which lies***
***This sprouting***
***Universe***

***Wherein***
***We are all a little concerned***
***And***

***Nervous.***

-Hafiz, translated by Daniel Ladinsky

I personally have found many clever ways to cope with these concerns, and frankly, Barry frequently has to remind me not to define the Mystery! He is more playful than I am, more surrendered to the delight of dancing with the Mystery. I, however, suffer under the illusion that I know stuff.

It seems strange to say that there are some dangers that go along with knowing too much. I realize it's not that I do, in fact, know too much, I just think I know too much. Do you know what Socrates said, soon before he died?

***"I know that I know nothing."***

Yikes! One of the most brilliant sages who ever lived saw that truth just before he died. Somehow, when I "think I know," I'm not as receptive to the messages that come to me. I'm not as alert or curious, and I don't seem to get as far or as deep in my meditations. When I am able to trust that what needs to come forth will, I am often surprised and delighted to uncover something I never suspected.

This is true for me if I am meditating on my own or with another person. Too much direction can get in the way. In my case I have had to temper certain kinds of "objective," "scientific" information with a sense of wonder and awe about the incredible capabilities of the body. I have witnessed these capabilities, which often seem miraculous. Bring science and mystery together with....you guessed it! The Breath!

[After watching the landing of men on the moon...]

***August gazed at the sky where the moon was rising, large and ghostly silver.***

***"Look at her good, Lily," she said, "'cause you're seeing the end of something."***

***"I am?"***

***"Yes, you are, because as long as people have been on this earth, the moon has been a mystery to us. Think about it. She is strong enough to pull the oceans, and when she dies away, she always comes back again."***

***August stared at the sky a long moment and then … said, "Now it won't ever be the same, not after they've landed up there and walked around on her. She'll be just one more big science project."***

-*The Secret Life of Bees* by Sue Monk Kidd

One time, I showed a film on the body (down to the cell level) to an on-going Cell Level Meditation class I was leading. One man was working on healing a bone that had fractured and wasn't healing properly. He'd had a stunning breakthrough one week! He saw color, energy, movement and was really able to get in with the healing breath. His pain level was minimal when he left that evening. It was the following week, when I showed the film. Then we did the meditation and he was so disappointed! He told me I'd ruined it for him. What was true and powerful and healing for him had come to him spontaneously, in a way that was meant for him. We each find our own way.

So cultivate "not knowing" and childlike curiosity—simply wonder—and let the softness of your gaze open up. Don't ruin the Mystery! And—be prepared for delightful surprises!

Having said this, understanding the "mechanics" of how something works can also be quite exhilarating. Biologists and Quantum Physicists are discovering all kinds of new information. We have imaging technologies that are confirming our inner "seeings." If you study a medical text about what's going on physiologically, it may open you to see things you wouldn't notice if the idea, image or concept hadn't been stimulated into your awareness by being exposed to it in a book. If you have diabetes, for example, studying all the dynamics of the pancreas, the production of insulin, and the responsiveness of the cells to glucose is a great idea. Just keep in mind that our bodies are amazing organisms that work with such intelligence, so we want to be cautious about limiting their creative and curative responses by our limited understanding of how they work to begin with.

I am reminded of Bruce Lipton's story of being ostracized by his colleagues when he discovered that the cell membrane has intelligence. In fact, he considers it the "brain" of the cell, instead of the nucleus! Bruce Lipton is a Cell Biologist who has discovered many of the things this book is about in the laboratory. However, when he tried to share this with his colleagues, the information threatened their world view of how they think things work and so they couldn't accept what he was showing them, yet...

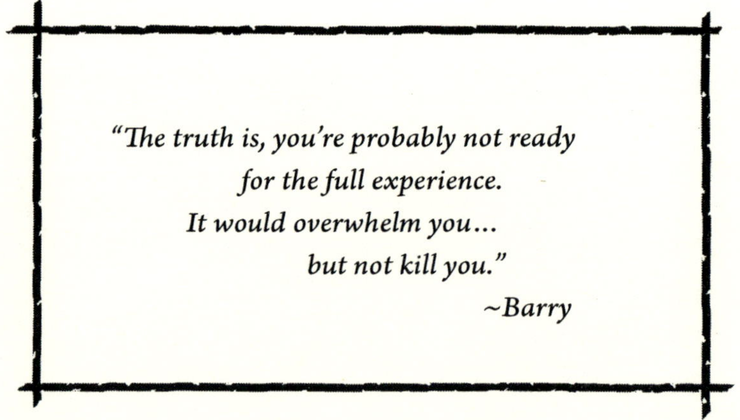

***"The truth is, you're probably not ready***
***for the full experience.***
***It would overwhelm you...***
***but not kill you."***
***~Barry***

# 7
# Falling? Dive!

***"And so accept everything which happens,***
***even if it seems disagreeable, because it leads to this:***
***the health of the universe...***
***For [Zeus] would not have brought on any man***
***what he has brought, if it were not useful for the whole."***

Marcus Aurelius
Roman Emperor, 121-180 AD

Whatever comes toward you as you take this journey inside your body, dive in. Once I talked to a guy who liked to climb rocks. He told me something very amazing. He said that one time when he was climbing, he fell. For a brief moment he experienced fear and then he moved beyond the fear and decided to go into the fall as if he were diving. And, he managed to land on the ground in a way that he didn't even get hurt.

Cell Level Meditation can be like this. Instead of recoiling in fear or helplessness, jump into whatever comes toward you. Ride the breath into it. Notice the sensation: the color, the sound, the smell, the feel, or the taste; take the breath into it; become it and breathe some more. Keep going!

So, breathe into your body with curiosity. Take the breath toward the cells. Go into whatever comes toward you. Trying to fix it and don't know what to do? Notice where that thought lives in your body, then breathe into the ***"trying to fix it."*** Breathe! If a sad cell comes toward you...hmm...what is your response? All the way inside, you find out who you are. And there's only one you in all the world. Use your own creative response to whatever is your true experience. Breathe to it!

If an evil cell comes toward you...hmm...what will you do? Now you may have to engage in such philosophical questions. And the cells and the breath may reveal some surprises that inform your life in interesting ways. I can tell you that wherever I have encountered evil, there has been a profound disconnect...like a disembodied mind that was not aware of its interconnectedness and interdependence with others. So, if you deal with cells that have no interest in being in relationship with other cells, you may need to restrain them and help the body activate ways to keep them from hurting the others, including moving them right on out of the body, or retraining them to be helpful (like the bacteria in the gut that helps digest our food, but is not allowed to get in the blood and wreck havoc). How you deal with such a deep question reveals the depths of your own nature.

It often happens that you begin Cell Level Meditation with the desire to heal something wrong with your physical health, but by breathing into what is given to you, fully experiencing what comes to you, you end up finding out who you really are and what you're good at or what's really important to you. Perhaps, this is how heaven and earth come together: the Spirit (the breath) comes into animate your embodiment as a human (earth). This is the true healing. And! Our bodies don't lie, so ***listen watchfully***! Take the breath to the place, quality or sensation the body points toward, and dive in there.

Now I will give you a little preview that you may find tantalizing. Consider:

> ***Barry says,***
>
> ***"Each cell is the same as every other cell. Then it changes and becomes whatever specialized cell is needed by the body."***

Each type of cell in the body has its own characteristics, but it also holds a certain basic and profound similarity with all cells. You may discover that bone cells have a different "feel" to them than, let's say, nerve cells. They store certain memories, hold certain patterns, and keep the structure solid. Nerve cells, carrying electrical impulses are more "zippy." So, since you are going into things as they are, taking the breath to them, becoming them, "matching" your breath to the sensations, you may find it useful to notice the speed or frequency something is expressing itself at. Then, slow down or speed up to "match" the speed so you can get in. The calcium in bones is much slower than the electricity of the nervous system.

Perhaps you are more tuned into sound. Some people hear tones and humming when they go in to their bodies. So, if you hear a tune, try matching your voice to it, just like listening to the concertmaster, who sounds the note on which everyone should start to sing. Listen for the note, and match your breath to it.

I'll give you an example. Once I tripped over a log and fell down flat on my stomach and chest. Immediately, I met the whole sensation exactly as it was, using my voice out loud. I stayed with this sensation for several minutes, using my breath/voice.

Now, if you think about having such a startling accident, you can imagine I wasn't chanting "Kumbaya," but rather the noise that came out of me was intense and almost primal, like an animal howling.

It seems that by meeting my true experience of the situation in this way, within minutes the pain and shock were gone. I got up and there was never any bruising, no after-effect of swelling, soreness or stiffness. Healing came about instantly. And if you think about it, perhaps this is why we spontaneously cry out, "Ouch!" when we hurt ourselves—it's a form of cell meditation!

The point is, if you experience something intense in your body, meet it with something equally intense. Instead of trying to calm yourself down, meet the intensity of what is happening, as it is happening. Go into it with curiosity: simply wonder. Become it and breathe, taking spaciousness into the center of it all. And remember Barry's words:

> ***"The truth is, you're probably not ready***
> ***for the full experience.***
> ***It would overwhelm you…***
> ***but not kill you."***
> ***~Barry***

# 8

# Emotions

***"Why look you,***
***how you storm!***
***I would be friends with you and have your love."***

William Shakespeare
playwright, 1564-1616

Sometimes, when you're traveling around in your body, you might come upon an emotional feeling. Of course, you know that the sensation you have inside when you're angry is different than when you're sad, which is different from loneliness or from excitement. It is tempting to go into thoughts about the emotion (why you think it is there).

***As Barry says,***
***"When you do that,***
***you separate the mind and the body."***

Try noticing the sensations ***in the body*** that the emotion evokes. That's where you go in. ***Become*** the sensation in the body, evoked by the emotion. Match your breath to the sensation and let Mystery do the rest. Perhaps a deeper healing is at hand. Breathe and breathe some more. Let the breath do the work!

Sometimes when you go into a meditative process engaging the cells, you may find yourself steeped in memories that evoke strong emotions. The cells seem to store our life histories, and I believe, the life histories of our ancestors. Because the larger intelligence of the body is always making the decision of what level of attention to engage when we go inside, we don't really know what will come forth.

Most people have a lot of opinions about "good" emotions they like to feel and "bad" emotions they don't think they're supposed to feel. So, sometimes, energy patterns can get trapped, clear down at the cell level. Let's say you're breathing and an old memory comes up. You see yourself as a child pouting in the corner, feeling sad and neglected. Some part of you is still there, feeling sad and neglected and the last thing you want to do is to stir up all the pain that's been numbed away for years.

However, right now you can go on a rescue mission and bring that child to safety. Go in and shout, "run for you life," and grab his or her hand and get him to safety. In this very moment, you're safe, right? So, in this moment ***by staying absolutely present with the breath*** you can go into a previous moment from this new place and help it shift. Allow a larger spaciousness around the experience and this helps to begin a transformative process so the sadness, little by little, (or, why limit ourselves? ***Once and for all!***) comes to resolution. Some awareness opens, some freedom comes, the minor key turns to the major resolution, or some release happens that allows for the energy held in a constricting pattern to become available for other uses. You may find that while the memory of the trauma is still there, it no longer holds you in the same way. And…this is also happening in the cell: energy has been released and made available for living with greater ease, freedom and creativity.

Traveling in this realm for healing purposes, especially where trauma is stored, can open new pathways and soothe old ones that are suffering from "hurt feelings." Take the breath to the cells over and over. The breath knows how to heal things. You don't have to know it all. Just take the breath into the body, into the sensations you experience, into the cells.

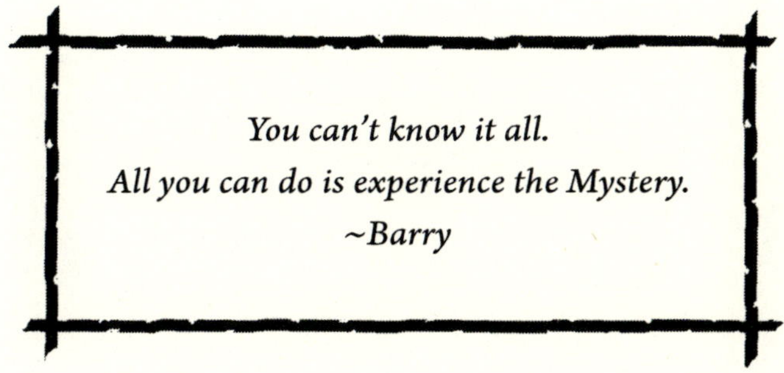

***You can't know it all.***
***All you can do is experience the Mystery.***
***~Barry***

Among the more poignant emotions is grief. Ahh! When grief arises, it too has a place in the body. Meeting this place, which the body reveals, with the mercy of the breath helps grief find the very alchemy by which healing actually happens even more deeply. This is different than thinking, "I just have to be cheerful."

On the contrary, you may find some very deep transformation by staying carefully present while the body is howling in lament, breathing into that, into the sensations, going into them just as you can with the breath, the merciful and powerful breath. You are staying present with the actual sensations in the body as the cells are transforming into greater intelligence.

Often, as something new is trying to emerge, something old has to die. Saying good-bye may bring up grief. If this is what is alive in the cell community, we listen for the sensations in the body that want and need the Merciful Breath.

*Breathing with joy*
*(and my feet begin to dance)*
*Howling with lament*
*(and my heart breaks open)*
*Roaring with anger*
*(and my confusion is burned to ashes)*
*Crouching in shame*
*(and my groveling shape-shifts to dignity)*

*Ha!*

*You just never know*
*what the*
*Great Mystery*
*will send*
*for your soul's release.*

# 9

# Being IN The Body—5 Senses & Beyond

***"A man will be imprisoned in a room with a door that's unlocked and opens inward, as long as it does not occur to him to pull rather than push."***

Ludwig Wittgenstein
philosopher, 1889-1951

By now, it should be obvious that Cell Level Meditation is directed toward being in the body. You are actually tuning into the body as an expression of creativity, vitality, health, and human experience. Many people think they're supposed to have far-out experiences or see celestial beings. And nothing like this happens. Well, of course, it can and does happen, but that's not what we're aiming toward.

Can you be present for exactly what is going on, just as you experience it? Can you stay with the breath as it travels inside your nose? Can you experience the pause between the in-breath and the out-breath? Can you stay "conscious" as you experience the sensation in your nose as the breath goes all the way out? If you can do this, you are a Zen Master!

And, it's also true, that as you turn your awareness into your body, you can, over time, have an experience—either visual, auditory or felt—of different body tissues. How the cells, organs and tissues make themselves known to you is just your way of perceiving things. Notice what comes to you, as it comes to you and breathe to that.

Since you have "programmed" yourself with a certain intention or purpose for doing the meditation, let your breath go toward the part of your body that needs some breath. If you are working on the bones, take the breath into the bones. If you are working on the skin, take the breath into the skin. If you are working on a healthy liver, take your breath into the liver. And so on.

So many things can happen as you do Cell Level Meditation. Sometimes, people think they can't meditate. Or they have ideas that they're supposed to see things or have certain experiences. You just never know what's going to happen.

The first time I went into my liver cells, everything turned bright orangey-yellow. Now this is a color that is associated with bile, something the liver makes. In herbal medicine, some of the plants that are known to help the liver are bright yellow, like the dandelion! So, I had a good time, breathing into yellow. A few people I've known have also had the experience of finding themselves "seeing" or "feeling" a certain color. By taking the breath into the color, we help the cells that seem to need that particular experience. The color energizes them or soothes them or tones them or helps them get rid of junk they don't need. So, if a color comes to you, breathe into it. Dive into it. Have a full experience of it.

*Blue*

*I look for the bluest blue*
*a winged blue*
*the most maritime*
*the blue alone*
*most encrusted in its blueness.*

*I look for the bluest blue*
*the most exquisite blue for my tongue*
*the blue that joins all the blues written in space*
*the blue that was here*
*when the wolf opened his eyes.*

*I look for the bluest blue*
*the most inexorable*
*the widest of all schools of fish blue*
*I look for the bluest trill, that converts all bluish trills*
*into one single blue note*

*I look for the bluest blue*
*that will make me shudder*
*in one eternal phrase, of blue*

-Ekiwah Adler-Beléndez,
reprinted with personal permission of the author

Now each color has its particular gifts and qualities. It is a manifestation of a frequency of light. You can find out about these frequencies yourself, by letting yourself open to the experience of them.

Another thing cells like to experience is sound. As you are traveling inside yourself on the wings of your breath, you may hear a kind of sound. Maybe it's a high-pitched buzz or a low-pitched ***humm***. Breathe into that sound and fully experience it.

One time, a very interesting meditation came out of a song that mysteriously came to me. So, I "breathed the song," which was about water. Guess which cells were wanting attention that day? Yes! The bladder cells got my attention by singing a "water song."

***Hey! Muscle Cell!***
***What do you want?***
***"Humm, humm, humm!"***
***So, I breathe,***
***"Humm, humm, humm!"***

As I do this, I notice a kind of enlivening. The color I'm seeing (in my mind's eye) becomes brighter. There is a kind of joyfulness. ***"Humm. Humm. Humm."*** You just never know what the cells are going to want on any given day!

Later that day, you may be surprised to hear a song on the radio that makes you feel enlivened. Go ahead! Breathe into it! Let your muscles have some fun by dancing! ***"Humm. Humm. Humm."***

Taste is another sense that the cells may use to get your attention. I have noticed that people have certain cravings for things that the cells need. So, if you discover the sensation of chocolate being alive in the body, that's the door in, taking the breath into the flavor, breathing into the flavor, becoming the flavor. Yum!

The sense of smell is said to evoke our deepest memories. Now it's true that the places our bodies want healing are stored in different levels of consciousness, or frequencies. Allowing ourselves to go deeply into the places in our cells where healing happens requires a letting go into altered states, almost like we're dreaming but participating in the dream.

So, if you find a smell arising, sniff your way into that place and allow it to show you where it wants a breath of fresh air! Go into the aroma, breathe in the beautiful roses that are bringing a Valentine present to your heart, and become that, breathe some more.

As you're breathing into your body, as you're paying attention to what's going on in your body, your five senses are speaking to you.

Images or colors (visual) may appear in your mind's eye; buzzing sounds may become prominent or the memory of a beautiful piece of music or your cat may meow (use everything!); or a smell seems to waft by; or you become aware of a certain flavor; you notice a tingle, a twitch or a rhythmic throb, the feel of velvet or prickly heat.

Notice, my friends, these are sensations in the body! We all have them! Just tune into what's there. Take your curiosity and awareness to what you actually experience. Take your breath into these sensations. Become these sensations. Breathe.

You may discover there's a lot more there than you thought. How you experience it has to do with how you're put together. Breathe to that!

Having mentioned that we have five senses that help us experience the world, in meditation, something happens, in which we shift into a different "state" of awareness, where the five senses seem to have some numinous quality that deepens our experience of wonder. We get the sense that there's something beyond what meets the eye (or the ear, nose, taste, touch or feel of things).

By noticing the sensations in the body with curiosity and breathing with them again and again, it may feel like you're going into a dream-world. In fact, the electrical frequency your brain works on when you are awake may change, like it does when you're dreaming.

Cell Level Meditation may be compared with Lucid Dreaming, in which you, the Dreamer, are actually participating in the Dream. "You" are staying awake for the dream of the body, learning to perceive within a new frequency or bandwidth of information storage. Your body stores things in all kinds of ways.

***Like a ripple***
***That chases the slightest caress***
***Of the breeze—***
***Is that how you want me***
***To follow you?***

-Ono No Komachi
Japanese poetess, ca. 834-?
translated by Jane Hirshfield with Mariko Aratani

Have you ever awakened with a vivid dream just as the phone was ringing? You spring out of bed and answer the phone. Your awareness shifts to your waking state, as you carry on a conversation with the caller.

After the phone call, you can't remember the dream. Poof! It's gone! It was so vivid, and now it's gone. If you wanted to find the dream again, you would have to shift back into the frequency of awareness you were in when you were in the dream.

It turns out we're multi-dimensional beings with many levels of information stored in different levels and layers of awareness or electro-magnetic frequencies.

Keep this in mind as you keep awareness "light" enough to find the frequency your healing intention requires.

And I will mention, it's not as difficult as you may think, to tune into these mysterious places. When children were asked what love is: Bobby, age 7, said:

"Love is what's in the room with you at Christmas if you stop opening presents and listen."

Yeah! Like that!

We get quiet and listen...the love is already there.

# 10

# Standing Back Far Enough to See

***"Every man takes the limits of his own field of vision for the limits of the world."***

Arthur Schopenhauer
philosopher, 1788-1860

Now, it's true, most of us have a bit of a challenge when we first sit down and try to become still to meditate. In our culture, we engage our minds so much, it's hard to turn them off sometimes. Some Buddhists refer to this "chatty" quality of our minds as "The Monkey Mind." So, another useful skill is developing the ability to watch "the show" or to become witness to the thoughts.

While it's true that sometimes the Monkey Mind takes over and you just get too fidgety to meditate once in awhile, and you may have to get up and go do something else and come back to it later. But! I have another clue for you! Take a step back from "Monkey Mind." Notice that something in you can watch your mind jumping around, thinking of this and that. You stand back from the picture to "see" it from a larger perspective. From this perspective, notice the "quality" of what's going on. Notice the "jumping-around-from-subject-to-subject-quality." Or notice the random "going-all-over-like-a-pinball-machine" quality. Notice the overall sensation of this as you begin to see what's going on in your body…and take the breath to that. Become that sensation. Breathe to that.

Breathe into "scattered."

Breathe into "floating all over."

Breathe into "can't settle down."

People are often surprised how familiar this sensation is. One man told me that his thoughts seemed random and that he couldn't concentrate. I told him to breathe into that. He was so surprised that this very sensation was so familiar to him—he never thought of going into it, since he'd spent so much of his life trying to avoid it. As he began to breathe toward what he described as "randomness," he found the door into to a deeper level of experience. And, perhaps it won't surprise you to learn that he discovered this kind of "randomness" further on down the line in his meditations…and his cells.

It is different to get lost in something like "randomness" than to go into it intentionally. Sometimes you have to bring yourself back gently to your intention or go back to the breath to stay in a meditative state and not just fall asleep. It is pretty common to get lost now and then. Remember: notice the sensations, take the breath into the sensations, become the sensations and keep breathing. With each breath you and your cells are discovering each other, negotiating, learning, communicating and getting to know each other.

Watching the "show" of your thoughts, which come and go, helps you to develop the Witness, the one who stands back and just observes. This can give you the larger perspective I just described, so you can take the breath to a larger movement that goes on inside of you.

I am going to describe a scenario that you have probably encountered if you've ever tried to do any meditation at all. You sit down to meditate and right away your mind kicks in with all kinds of thoughts, commentary and lists of things to do. Now the "Witness" is asked to notice not just the thoughts, but also the quality behind the thoughts and the sensations in the body where this quality might be identified. The minute you sit down, the mind often shows up. You are breathing, in and out, and suddenly up on the screen of the mind comes a thought:

***"Oh, I must remember to get bread at the store."***

Now there probably isn't a lot of emotional charge associated with this thought, so you can just notice it showed up and go back to breathing, in and out, in and out. Then another thought comes,

***"Oh, also soap, I need to get soap."***

And on the heels of this thought, another thought intervenes, saying,

***"You idiot! Can't you just shut up and be silent? You're supposed to be meditating, damn it!"***

Now, if we step back in these easy-to-imagine scenarios, there is a feeling or a felt sense about each of these scenarios, no? In the first thought, there's probably not a lot of energy or "charge." You probably don't have strong feelings about such a thought, right? So, in the body, things are still fairly neutral. Not much is going on.

In the second thought, the judgmental thought, there might be quite a bit of energy. It may evoke strong feelings. These feelings show up as an experience ***in the body***. Where is this energy in the body? Is there tightness in the jaw? Tension in the shoulders? Wherever and whatever the sensation is, take the breath to it. Become that sensation.

This is the active part of the meditation. You're not falling asleep; you're not being swept away in your usual thought processes; you're noticing and sensing exactly what comes to you, the feeling in the body or how you perceive it. Then, you go into it. You take the breath into it. You become it. You are going beyond the thoughts, into the underlying energy in the thoughts, diving in through the place beyond your mind.

And, guess what? All of this happens at the cell level. You experience the cells in the best way your psyche knows how to get your attention!

*The Guest House*

*This being human is a guest-house*
*Every morning a new arrival.*

*A joy, a depression, a meanness,*
*Some momentary awareness comes*
*As an unexpected visitor*

*Welcome and entertain them all!*
*Even if they're a crowd of sorrows,*
*Who violently sweep your house*
*Empty of its furniture,*

*Still, treat each guest honorably.*
*He may be clearing you*
*Out for some new delight.*

*The dark thought, the shame, the malice,*
*Meet them at the door laughing,*
*And invite them in.*

*Be grateful for whoever comes,*
*Because each has been sent*
*As a guide from beyond.*

-Rumi
Sufi poet and mystic, 1207-1273
translated by Coleman Barks

# 11

## Meditating with Nature

***Watching the moon***
***At dawn,***
***Solitary, mid-sky,***
***I knew myself completely,***
***No part left out.***

Isumi Shikibu
Japanese poetess., 970-?
translated by Jane Hirschfield with Mariko Aratani

Turning the attention to something larger than yourself, something you recognize as already Whole and beautiful and good, helps you remember and realign with your own Wholeness (the word from which 'health' comes). Great herbalists report being able to tune toward a plant and to ask it what it heals. Being a little denser than these great healers, I have to fall back on my experience of nature. Looking at a plant, I get silent. Then I notice what response I get in my body by gazing on this plant. What sensations can I notice?

Sometimes, I have to become more silent (go deeper into no-thing) before I can notice what sensations the plant evokes in me. I breathe into this sensation. I discovered a deep sense of calm by breathing toward the velvety darkness in the inner chamber of a tulip. Over the next few days, I found myself going back to this velvety silence that I experienced as calming, and my whole body would become relaxed and peaceful.

One autumn, I got a very bad cough, and my trachea, or windpipe, felt very irritated. I realized after a week or so that I was very drawn to breathe toward the trees that lined the roads where I live. I breathed in the trees and noticed my windpipe seemed to enjoy it. But there's more—without really thinking about it, I was determined to line my driveway with two-foot logs, standing up, to make a little barrier between the gravel and the grass.

It didn't occur to me what my psyche was up to until I happened to be reading about columnar cells in an anatomy textbook. It turns out that there are cells in the trachea that are standing up in columns (columnar cells) and they kind of guard this tube into the lungs by helping stop dust particles and bacteria.

Aha! Maybe that's why I'd been breathing toward the trees and making little stand-up barriers. Certainly the irritation eased off and I got better.

In nature (and in our lives) there is usually something right in front of us, re-minding us, showing us how healing is coming about in our bodies. So, look around and see what you are drawn to breathe into.

*Your mind-body loves metaphors;*
*It's a poet, you know.*
*It likes seeing how one thing is like another,*
*Like how tall pines along the road*
*Are like the columnar cells*
*Along the road to the lungs.*
*Breathe to that!*

# 12

## Resistance

***"A clash of doctrines is not a disaster—it is an opportunity."***

Alfred North Whitehead
philosopher, 1861-1974

Sometimes you may find yourself irritable, skeptical and doubtful. Oh, these clever tricksters who try to keep you from your heart's desire! Now you may have to be very clever on occasion! You may have to get into the coyote skin and, unnoticed, slink by the monster that says, "You can't do this!" You may have to tiptoe by him or slip by when his back is turned.

Some people are able to take the breath to these feelings. I knew one young man who was very aware of ***not*** wanting to get well. He felt embarrassed to admit it, but every time he had to do physical therapy, he just came up against his resistance.

So, one day, he decided to explore it. He breathed into the resistance. Before long, he found himself in a meditative state, floating around in water, and it was quite blissful. Suddenly, ***boom***! The water rushed out and he was being born...prematurely. He was so angry with that! He really wanted to be back in that blissful, warm water of his mother's womb. You know what he did? He spent several sessions in the bliss of the water. He found it calmed something in him and the resistance to doing the physical therapy decreased.

As you may notice from reading about this fellow's resistance or remembering some experience you've had with –

NOT WANTING THINGS TO BE THE WAY THEY ARE,

you may notice there can be a lot of energy stored in this. Since part of the mind's job is to notice things, it can notice where this energy is stored and how much energy is invested in this tantrum. It can ask if this tantrum is serving your well-being or not. But first you must notice that you're having an inner tantrum about –

NOT WANTING WHAT YOU HAVE TO DEAL WITH!

This alone may be liberating.

This tantrum may be stored more as a "whine." Why me? Just feel the "why me?" That's resistance. I remember another young man with a lot of psychological training. He had a lot of insight into himself, and these insights sometimes turned into excuses that didn't really serve him all that well. He discovered an idea he had that he was "too hard on himself." Trying to counter this "idea," gave him an excuse to stay in bed every morning in a way that left him a little lethargic all day. His resistance to getting up at a time which allowed him to take a walk wasn't really serving him, since he'd discovered through his own experiments that he felt better and had more energy when he actually got up and got his walk in. So, "too hard on himself" was an idea. The actual experience, in the body may be another way through to a deeper aliveness. In his case, he discovered at times, he needed to be a little harder on himself!

These things are pretty tricky. You can see how convoluted the path can be at times.

So, resistance? First find it. If you can, breathe to it.

And! Like Odysseus on his journey homeward, use every trick in the book!

# 13
# Breathing to Beliefs

***"A belief is not merely an idea the mind possesses;
it is an idea that possesses the mind."***

Robert Bolton
author, as quoted in the London Guardian

You may discover deep beliefs that seem to live (or possess you) in your body, all the way down at the level of the cells. One woman I know, for example, inherited both the physical tendency and the mental tendency of perfectionism. In Cell Level Meditation, she got to the very core of this "structure." She found cells that were "perfect," absolutely sterile and mechanical. They were all the same. She had complained bitterly about her upbringing with a mother that treated her and her siblings in exactly the "same" way. They were all dressed alike, given the same foods to eat and so on.

Now, at the very core of her she found the same tendency, expressed at a cellular level. She had to breathe into her pain about that. She went into the cells and began to pay attention to them and to tune into what seemed good for them and to distinguish what felt right from what she intellectually thought was right in a perfectionist way. She was able to question her beliefs about conformity and perfectionism and become more fluid in the moment's requirements of her. Outwardly and inwardly there was more fluidity of response.

You may discover pain that needs to be healed, values you need to uphold, your strengths, and your fears. And you discover what is truly healing as you take the breath to the cells. You may find something startlingly familiar as you find yourself traveling into the cells. You can ask yourself, "Where else have I experienced this?" Try not to get stuck in the story and keep breathing creatively. Distinguish between mind and body and bring breath to the body's sensations now. Become those sensations. Breathe some more. Participate in the Mystery, instead of thinking about it. Dance, instead of thinking about which foot goes left, and which foot goes right.

You may find yourself angry about being sick or trying to find out why you're sick. Hey, you don't really know why you're sick. No one knows. Having an illness is so mysterious. But, here it is. You want to get better. If you're angry about being sick, breathe into the anger! Mine the energy in the anger and use it to rally your healing response.

I worked with a fellow who had terrible problems with emphysema—he was shocked to discover something he couldn't let himself acknowledge. He really believed he was incurable. This was so hidden to him, since he'd spent years and lots of money on lots of different therapies, but there it was as plain as day when he breathed toward his lungs: a recalcitrant belief that he was incurable. I must say, in his case, he didn't have a lot of help from the collective belief system. Lots of people think emphysema is incurable. Now he didn't want to believe he was incurable, but this is what he found cemented into body and reinforced by everyone he knew.

If you find yourself believing your illness is some kind of punishment, notice where that lives in your body and breathe to that. Acknowledge your belief. Maybe you have to make amends somewhere. Or maybe you have to breathe to a belief that no longer serves you, and let it loosen its hold on you, and say, "Be gone!"

***"Dost thou think because thou art virtuous, there shall be no more cake and ale?"***

-William Shakespeare

You may be surprised to find beliefs or emotions that are relics from the past, from your ancestors. One day, I discovered a deep sense of homesickness and I had a brief glimpse of getting off a boat and feeling overwhelmed. My grandparents were immigrants to the US, and it came to me that this homesickness I've known all my life as a vague sense was something that came down to me from my grandmother. (Oh, I see you are laughing that I started this book with a story about a guy who is trying to get home! There's just no hiding from ourselves, no?)

Everything that you can become aware of is a place for exploration, a place to discover and toward which you can take the breath. Beware of getting caught up in analyses or explanations—just be honest with what you experience and … breathe to the sensation it evokes in you in the body. Take healing breath, holy spirit, to the body and let it all come into healing.

In the process of doing this, you become a more vibrant expression of the Life Force that lives through you. Yes, you! You are the unique and creative expression of something very mysterious. Cell Level Meditation helps you discover yourself way down deep.

Gradually, a sense of this marvelous life force that ***is*** you begins to evoke awe and respect. Then true self-confidence and self-esteem may be born. Not because you're ***supposed*** to have self-confidence, but because you have touched something inside yourself that you know is beautiful and wonderful, and quite naturally, you want to live in harmony with it. It feels real to you. You become a co-participant with Life, rather than a victim or a tyrant. This may happen because you are more consciously aware of what is true for you.

# 14

# Treatments & Medication, Vitamins & Herbs

***"As a sweet apple turns red on a high branch
high on the highest branch and the apple pickers forgot—
well, no, they didn't forget—were not able to reach..."***

Sappho
Greek lyric poetess, ca. 630-570 BC
translated by Anne Carson

Consider for a moment, that all kinds of messengers are arriving at the door of the cell, all the time. The cell can say, "Hey, come in," or, "Go away," or, "Come back later." While we often have the idea that this is a fairly mechanical process, there is something more at work...in the gap...where you can let the breath, a prayer, an intention, or words of encouragement in. So, if you are taking medications, a homeopathic remedy, vitamins, herbs or receiving some kind of treatment for an illness, use Cell Level Meditation to focus and enhance the treatment.

Take a few moments to get quiet and go into silence. Tune into your body. Tune into your intention for taking the medication or treatment. Let your body know that help for healing is on the way. Sense your body's response to this and breathe. Breathe to the cells, "Help is on the way!"

As you take the medication, use your breath to direct it to the purpose for which it's intended. Whisper in the ear of the attack dog, "Sic 'em! Go get those cancer cells (or viral cells or whatever-illness cells)!" Maybe you'll feel protective of your healthy cells. Listen in and breathe toward their protection. Shield them for any noxious side effects.

***Breath to cells.***
***Breathe! Breathe! Breathe!***
***You don't have to know how to do it all.***
***Take in the breath, the Mighty Breath.***
***May you benefit completely.***
***May the benefit be great.***
***May the benefit be completely great.***

A teacher I knew made a trip around the world. He was a little nervous about getting sick in countries where sanitation systems weren't as sophisticated as he was used to. When he got to these countries, he would put his hands on his stomach before eating. He'd notify his body that food was coming and that lots of people ate this food and benefited from it. He'd tune in and let his body know it could find a healthy relationship with the food. He never got sick.

This same man could also go to the vitamin section of a store and ask his body if any particular vitamin would benefit him. He could sense what he needed and what he didn't need. As you get better at tuning into yourself, this won't seem strange to you. Tune in and "listen" (sense, feel or "see," according to your way of tuning in) for your body's response to food, vitamins, medications and whatever else you take into yourself. Hmmm, sounds like a way to be more conscientious in general, no?

I know another woman who decided to get chemotherapy for cancer. She was very worried about the toxic effect of this treatment on the healthy cells of her body. She went into meditation, and gave her healthy cells little yellow rain slickers, so they would be protected from the "acid rain" of the chemotherapy. Whenever she went to get the infusion of chemotherapy, the healthy cells put on their rain slickers, and received protection. She had very few side-effects from chemotherapy, her choice of healing.

# 15

# Only One You—Creativity & Originality

***"Flee with thy life if thou fearest oppression***
***and leave the house to tell its builder's fate.***
***Thou wilt find, for the land that that thou quittest, another,***
***But no soul wilt thou find to replace thine own."***

One Thousand and One Nights

And you will also be creative! Be original. Go into everything with all of who you are. Try things on and throw them out. Notice what seems true to ***you***! Just breathe to the cells, to the sensations you experience, to what you are aware of. Just breathe! Experience everything fully. And, in your creativity, you may be moved to sing to your cells. I love lullabies, and as a mother or perhaps due to years of working with mothers and babies as a midwife, the feeling of tenderness is fairly well-developed in me. So, sometimes when I am breathing toward some cells that seem to want comfort, I sing a lullaby to them. I "breathe" the lullaby toward them. "There, there, little cells. Mom's here, you're going to be alright."

Do you like to dance? Once in a cell meditation I was exploring some feelings of anger I found in some cells, and on the breath I brought in a troupe of Flamenco dancers to "match" the sense of outrage I discovered in my body. My cells really enjoyed that one! The cells have rhythm too!

A woman I worked with saw the black image of death that came to her in a meditation session. She couldn't get rid of it, so she told it to get to work on the cancer cells in her body. Pretty gutsy!

A young man, who was just discovering young women, had to work on the myelin sheaths around his nerves. He found himself imagining a beautiful girl pulling on her stocking.

*Barry told me about a man he worked with who was an expert on the human eye. He was able to re-engineer his own eyes and regain his sight! Now that's focus! And he was quite motivated because he really wanted, just yearned to see the face of his wife.*

*Barry also had a client who breathed to his liver and he discovered the liver was a factory. So, he found a way to make the factory work better.*

*Another woman Barry worked with had to create white blood cells to survive, and she set up a factory with the seven dwarfs, who were singing all the time, "Whistle while you work."*

If you are a miner, you might find yourself mining the energy from a pattern to make it available for something else. If you are an engineer, you might find yourself re-wiring the circuitry of something that seems "off" to you.

As you explore all of these avenues of your own experience, my advice is to be creative, use your breath, and stay present with your own experience until you sense things are "in order" for that session.

How long does it take for things to heal? There is no simple way of answering this. A true healer would say things are already healed, and how long it takes you to remember that depends on your nature or fate or who knows? Things can heal in an instant! I know of one fellow who worked for 3 years to fully recover. Some cells in the body seem to act faster than others.

Maybe it's easier to get into some kinds of body cells for you than for others. Some cells are speedy and some are slow. Match the speed as you become the sensation. Maybe an instant healing would be too frightening for you because it would challenge everything that you hold dear, so it might be easier to heal a little at a time.

Mostly, our healing is impeded by our conditioning. If you've lived with something for a long time, you've made all kinds of allowances for this, and a pattern of compensation gets set up in the whole body, the nervous system and the brain. You can have an amazing breakthrough, and then you may have to practice getting used to being healthy. Once I healed a chronic knee problem and I noticed I was waiting for the problem to come back rather than enjoying and stabilizing the healed sensation. I had gotten so used to dealing with my bad knee that I didn't know how to be with my good knee. I had to practice.

So, in the spirit of integration and the experience of being human, it seems like an on-going practice is useful for many people. It just seems to take time to get in, to integrate the experience, to make it solid and stabilize it, and to realize, ***"My God! This stuff works!"***

***"The fox has his den, and the bird has his nest, but the Son of Man has nowhere to rest his head."***

-Matthew 8:20

Being human, we are told there is no dogma that can tell us how to meet every situation that comes up. But we do have the breath! That's the great tool in this meditative practice. And that brings us back to the Mystery, back to the spaciousness around us. Our own lives have come out of that Mystery, and can be healed, reprogrammed, and realigned when we turn toward a sense of newness to every moment by watching, listening, sensing into the situation and diving in with our own instincts and awareness and delight.

Of course you will discover this on your own. Perhaps you will try using something that "worked" for you yesterday, and today it flops. Or maybe it won't! There's just no dogma that always works, no place to rest your head. You are unique and different among all people. Whatever you are given is yours to bring to the moment. This is a paradox. On one hand, I'm suggesting that you come to the meditation, breath or moment with newness and freshness, and on the other, I'm telling you to bring all of who you are to the moment. Yes, both of these statements are useful tools! There is just no place where we can rest our heads!

In general, I would venture to say, that we get out of our "heads" when we do Cell Level Meditation. Instead of analyzing your experience, ***go into it*** with the breath. Simply wonder. Many things will come to us to engage: dreams, thoughts, beliefs, emotions, memories, visual images, sounds, smells, and so on. Instead of thinking about what comes to you or wondering "why or how or what does it mean," my best advice is to ask, "***Where*** is it in the body?" Go into the sense of it (as it comes to ***you***), take the breath into it and became that.

We're all curious about why things are the way they are. (And, as I mentioned, the "whys" can get you!) If we go into our heads too fast, we may not find out the deeper, more satisfying answers that end up connecting us way beyond what we could imagine. So, if you find yourself in very familiar territory, ***notice*** that it's familiar, and keep going!

# 16
# Experiencing The Cells

***"Go sit in your cell and your cell will teach you everything."***

Ascribed to one of the Desert Fathers
Christian monks who lived mainly in the
Scetes Desert of Egypt, ca. 3rd century

And you may be wondering, but what about the cells? This is Cell Level Meditation! Yes, we can get all the way down to the cells. In fact, anything that you are doing or thinking is also, in some way, going on in the cells, no?

Everything ultimately is a pattern of energy in expression. The manifest form, if you travel into it, is made of smaller parts, the smaller parts are made of even smaller parts, and so on, until you get down to a level where there is only the sensation of something like vibrancy itself arising from the emptiness. The expression of the energy of a substance running at a certain rate is solid, at another rate it's liquid, and at another it's a gas.

Every known substance has its parameters, temperature, rate and rhythm, and how it behaves under different circumstances. Similarly, different types of cells in the body have their own "signature" pattern of color, movement, speed, sound or energetic frequency. Muscle cells have a different kind of pattern than bone cells. And they "feel" different than bone cells in some kind of subjective way. The cells are working along with their own programming, and if you are suffering from an illness, you might find a sense of unease or disturbance when you get there. How do we work with that? Breathe to it! Become it! Be responsive. Just keep breathing. Stay curious and simply wonder how to engage the experience fully, looking for clues.

Now, because I have worked in health care, I had to study such things as biology and anatomy and physiology. So, I have seen the pictures of cells in textbooks and under the microscope. However, the first time I "saw" the cell membrane in Cell Meditation, I was quite moved. It was much more dynamic than I had imagined, and beautiful! A few years later, I was delighted to see a photo of a cell membrane taken with the use of an electron microscope, and I was pretty excited to have my vision corroborated. A couple of times I have had something like this happen. Once I got to a structure in my body that somehow I identified as a virus. It was very resistant to being in relationship with the other cells. In fact, it felt very "other," or foreign to me. A few weeks later, I went to pick up a friend at a doctor's appointment. While I was in the waiting room, waiting for her, I picked up a magazine, and there on the cover was a picture of the virus I'd seen, taken under an electron microscope!

Sometimes, I've noticed that the "cellular picture" comes as a metaphor. For example, one patient I worked with had some problems with her cholesterol levels, and when she went in, she described to me some pipes. As her description became more vivid and dynamic, I realized she was in the cardiovascular system, working on the plaque on the wall of blood vessels that needed some attention.

Other times, some people I've worked with and I have gone into the structure of the cell. There is a kind of geometry with shapes, color, movement and vibrancy. Participating in the harmony and beauty of this underlying pattern is an experience of great delight.

And! The potential that lies within you may astound you! The cells of the body are quite versatile, noble and capable of transformation (just like you are)! You have probably heard a little about stem cells. These are cells that haven't been programmed yet for a specific job.

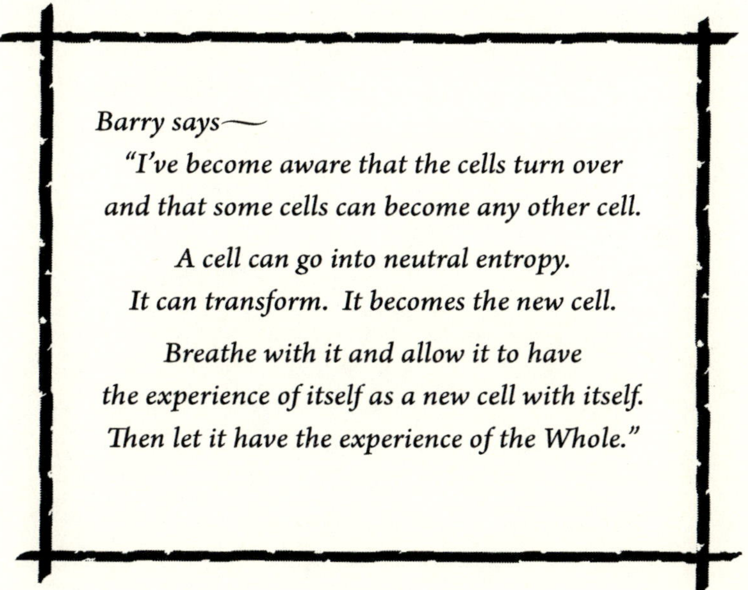

*Barry says—*

***"I've become aware that the cells turn over and that some cells can become any other cell.***

***A cell can go into neutral entropy. It can transform. It becomes the new cell.***

***Breathe with it and allow it to have the experience of itself as a new cell with itself. Then let it have the experience of the Whole."***

Whatever you can imagine, opens possibilities that can birth into physical reality. The noble cells of your body can rest, take stock of the situation and create solutions to problems. They can transform. They use creative solutions. In addition to their versatility, what makes the cells of the body so successful is their ability to cooperate! Sounds like we should be taking classes from them.

# 17

## Prayer

*Within the silence*
*of the silence*

*Just when you think you can't bear it another minute*
*And the ache of longing in your chest is beyond belief*
*And the lump in your throat is stinging your ears*
*And the howling of your yearning ends in silence*

*Within the silence*
*of that silence*

*A new heaven opens.*

Patricia Kay

For me, prayer is an experience of becoming silent, feeling into the stillness, and from there, up comes the statement, the request, the affirmation of healing, the thankfulness, the deep reverence of the experience of something very beautiful and holy.

When you feel toward your intention, and let it come alive in you, it is a kind of prayer. It comes from this very still place deep inside. When you pray for someone or yourself, be still, be silent, and let your heart's desire well up.

Put words to it. Music to it, and...breathe to it. This is another way to experience Cell Level Meditation. You start breathing into the place that needs healing, and you take the breath there like a blessing. "Here you go, little cell, some healing, healing breath for you. Be well."

And this arose from the silence from which surged the deep yearning to be Whole. Stay with it. A little longer. Keep going. Don't stop the Mystery!

And for the scientists among you, I mention that since 2000, at least ten studies of intercessory prayer have been carried out by researchers at institutions including the Mind/Body Medical Institute, a nonprofit clinic near Boston run by a Harvard-trained cardiologist, as well as Duke University and the University of Washington.

The results all seem to point toward the fact that "there's something to it." Dr. Larry Dossey has shown the power of prayer to work in double-blind studies.

Dr. Lewis Mehl-Madrona has been working with mind-body healing since the 80's. His grandmother was a Cherokee Indian, and as part of his fullness he brought Native American healing techniques to his medical practice. He has done research on the effects of prayer with patients who are recovering from surgery. He has found compelling evidence that shows that praying for others can accelerate their healing. Dr. Mehl-Madrona says,

*"We're presenting the idea that the brain is a sensory organ for spiritual phenomena. The EEG knows when you're being prayed for even if the patient does not. Medical science seems to be showing us quite graphically that we are all connected to each other and to the larger world."*

# 18

# Conditioned Habits

***"I hate television. I hate it as much as I hate peanuts. But I can't stop eating peanuts."***

Orson Welles
actor, writer, director, producer, 1915-1985

I love computers. They really show us so much about ourselves, since it was humans, after all that discovered the principles that made them work and invented and produced them. Computers are programmed to do many things. In a similar way, we are programmed. Now, if I want to change the programming in my computer, I can't just yell at it and say, "Hey, change the font I'm writing with." No, I have to find the program in the computer, go there, and see what options are available and make the changes. Sometimes I have to get new software! And some things can't be changed or the computer doesn't work at all. In a similar way, Cell Level Meditation, is a way of finding the programming and deciding if it's producing my current well-being or not.

What is really shocking is discovering just how unaware I am of most of my programming. Becoming aware that there is conditioned awareness and the body is responding to deep commands that in many cases have not been questioned is a discovery that most people have during the course of their healing journeys.

Programming can work in a positive way by using imagination and working with a guided visualization that you or someone else makes for you. These can be very powerful if they speak to you deeply. Many people benefit from these healing offerings. Barry and I have seen people derive great benefit from guided imagery. And people have asked, "Hey, where does that fit in all of this?" I personally believe that whatever creates a coherent field of awareness is useful for healing. Sometimes, we're uninspired. Sometimes, we're scared to death. Neither of these places is particularly conducive to healing. So, if you have the opportunity to be guided by someone you trust and admire through healing visualizations, this comes to you as a gift!

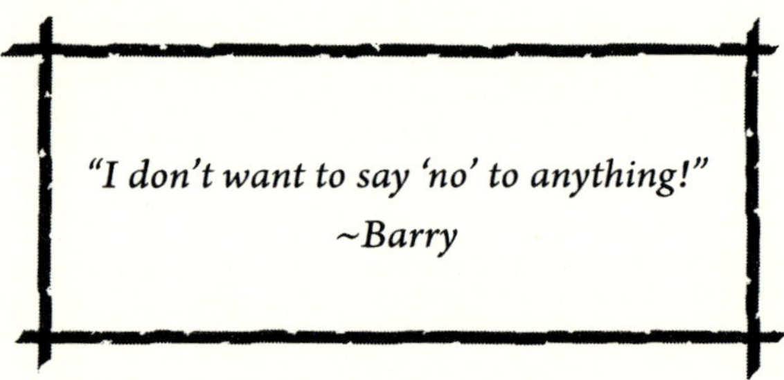


Use what speaks to you deeply, where your cells say, "Yes!" And listen deeply, more deeply, into the silence now for the cells to let you know about their true and deepest needs, their most beautiful expression of a Wholeness and loveliness of being that is their unique expression.

Once, I worked with a young man who was born with cerebral palsy. He had to have surgery to correct severe scoliosis of the spine. It was a very difficult surgery and he had to spend months in rehabilitation. During that time, we did Cell Level Meditation by phone. We had to recreate new neural pathways for certain muscles. It came to me to become aware of the nerve/muscle junction as I was in meditation.

Oh! This was delightful! I experienced a sense of electricity being received and responded to with matter! It seemed like a very joyful interchange. This was already happening in my own body, which I hoped could be a template for his, so his body could "reboot" and reprogram.

In the meantime, he was having his own experiences: noticing, breathing and becoming what came to him. He reported that after his sessions, which we did long-distance, he was able to stand up without pain for longer and longer periods. How much of this was conscious, and how much just happened because of the Mystery… well, I wouldn't know!

# 19

# Meditating with Others: The Cell Community

***"I am a success today because I had a friend who believed in me, and I didn't have the heart to let him down."***

Abraham Lincoln,
U.S. President, 1809-1865

All of the Great Wisdom traditions throughout the world speak of our interconnectedness. The cells live in community to make the body. Mostly, this community of cells gets along splendidly, with the liver doing its most excellent work, the kidneys doing their wonderful cleansing, the toes doing their tiptoeing, and so on. We have spoken about how each cell performs these functions. We have mentioned that cells, while performing all these functions, also begin to specialize and form a community with other like-minded cells to form organs that are dedicated to a specialty area, like getting blood pumped around (the heart) or transmitting messages (the nerves) or ridding the body of waste (the large intestine). The organ communities each work in a larger community, which we recognize as the body. What happens when these bodies (each consisting of trillions of cells) come together with other human bodies with the intention of being healthy? When we bring bodies together with shared intention, new levels of possibilities open up.

*Become aware of the liver cell.*
*Breathe to it.*
*Become aware of the experience of your liver cell.*
*Breathe.*
*Let the liver cell experience that you are there.*
*Let the liver cell experience itself as itself.*
*Open the panorama.*
*Breathe.*
*Let the liver cell experience itself*
*as part of the community of liver cells.*
*Breathe.*
*Now let the community experience itself as a*
*community.*
*Breathe.*
*And now let the community of liver cells experience*
*their part*
*of the larger community of the Whole Body.*
*Breathe.*
*Breathe.*

*~Barry*

The Buddhists talk about waking up to the false notion of ourselves as separate from each other. Then there's Jesus, who said it in another way: "Where two or more are gathered, there I ***am***." I take this to mean there is a kind of consciousness there that is different from being alone, and this goes all the way down to what's happening in the cells.

There are potentials for healing that we are just beginning to discover. Imagine: First, I am learning to listen to no-thing, then I am learning to listen to some-thing. Then I am breathing and listening to a dialogue, and I am surprised at what happens in this listening, this breathing and then becoming. In a similar way, I am listening to "me-ness," and then listening to "you-ness," and because of this, something new arises in awareness, mind and body.

Perhaps you've had your own experience of the heightened power of meditation when you are with another person or in a group. Someone further down the road in consciousness, awareness, or healthfulness can help shine the light on your own path. Your dance teacher shows you how to turn your foot in a little, and suddenly you can do the dance. Even so, as you walk the path or dance the dance, you have to make it your own.

Cell Level Meditation is deceptively simple. It just doesn't occur to us to breathe to the most obvious things that are so familiar we just can't see them. This is where others can help us. And it's also true that there seems to be something mysterious that happens when "two or more are gathered," and you meditate with another person. A higher energy level seems to be available that may be difficult to access on your own, so you may learn more, come to awareness faster, transform in ways you don't tend to do when you're by yourself. One fellow I know said, "I've transformed more in the last year and a-half [by being in an intentional group] than by doing 10 years of Buddhist meditation."

And, as I mentioned, our conditioning is so deep and much of it is out of our field of awareness! To help ourselves beyond the blind spots, sharing this kind of meditation with others can be very helpful.

Kabir, from India, was a 15th Century Poet or a divine smart aleck, as his translator Daniel Ladinsky calls him. He said:

***"The fish***
***That is thirsty***
***Needs serious***
***Professional Counseling."***

We are all like this fish in some ways, and our friends can be "serious professional counselors" because they see us in ways that are often hidden to us. Once, my friends made a comment that startled me, "You're really intense." They were as shocked to realize I didn't know this about myself as I was to discover it and begin to explore "intensity." Of course, my humanity of wanting to please people has tried to "correct this intensity," and then my friends say, "we like your intensity." So, I was glad to be aware of it, to discover where it was living in my body, to breathe with it, and to become it. And on and on goes the dialogue, the unfolding, the liberating, the new possibilities, the healing of old wounds, and the co-creation of a new edge of human potential and evolution.

Since we are each the fish in the fishbowl of our lives, looking for water, our friends can gently say things like, "You look scared!" You can try on what they're saying. Scared? Oh, yes! Where is that in my body? Breathe to it. Become it. And bring your friends along. They'll all benefit.

By sharing our experiences, and "breathing" with each other, very powerful healings can and do happen. If one person's immune system has already healed from some difficult disease, we now know this is humanly possible. Furthermore, by sitting in the field or presence of this person, our own immune systems are similarly inspired, primed and trained in new ways. When Roger Bannister ran the four-minute mile, soon after he broke through the limitation that said, "No one can run a mile under four minutes," many runners began to run that fast and then even faster!

Many medical centers have noticed that patients get better faster from diseases like cancer if they attend support groups. The principles created in the 12-Step Recovery Groups, like Alcoholics Anonymous, are very powerful in aligning the power of the group for healing.

And, each group also has something like a center of gravity where the participants agree on shared reality. I am reminded of a childbirth instructor who spent a lot of time educating her clients about all the things that could go wrong with them in their births, ostensibly to take their fears away. However, she had a high percentage of women who ended up having cesareans! Somehow they were all programmed to have things go wrong.

So, notice whether your support group helps you move to a higher center of gravity, a higher level of functioning or if it is programming you with limiting fears or pulling you down!

It's also true that sometimes we need to borrow faith from those who have a bit more experience than we do. This is just part of being human. Faith, by the way, isn't just wishful thinking, but rather a deeply felt knowing, usually from lived experience, that something is so.

Of course, if you've had some experience in achieving results at something, your mind is primed and open to repeating the results. Until you've had your own experience, "borrowing faith" from someone who has had the experience is not a bad idea.

We have to be gentle to start with so we're not tromping around in each other's sacred places, and causing harm. However, once trust develops in a meditation group, people can point out something that's so familiar to you, you missed it and never thought to go into it for transformative purposes.

Forming communities of Cell Level Meditators could be an important part of health care in the future, since it would engage our creativity, enhance our growing awareness of the mind/body connection, as well as make us aware of our inter-connectedness with each other, with matter and therefore with our environment.

Be the first on your block to start a Cell Level Meditation Group! The instructions are simple:

● 1. Notice the vast spaciousness around you.

■ 2. Notice what's going on in the body.

▲ 3. Take the breath from spaciousness into the sensation and become that.

● ▲ ■ 4. Keep going, noticing, breathing, becoming.

Breath to Body! Who knows what wonderful thing wants to happen through you and you and you?

One final word. When it ***does*** happen...breathe to it! Become it! Breathing into gratitude and wonder keeps the Mystery alive in you.

If you've been sick, it's easy to get into a rut of how much work is involved in getting better. You have to break this habit too.

Take the next breath into:

- JOY (breathe and become joy)
- DELIGHT (breathe and become delight), and
- VIBRANT HEALTH!

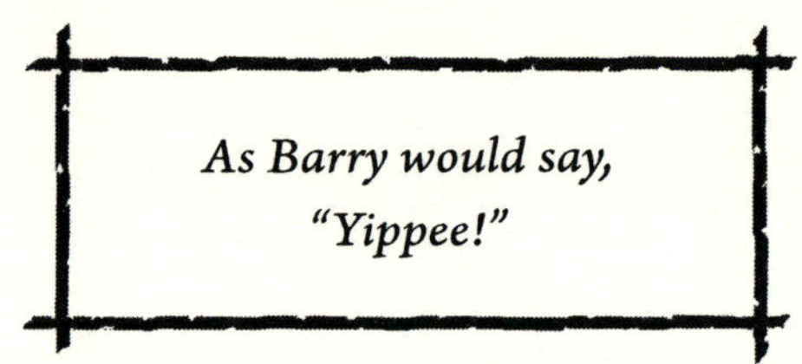

*As Barry would say,*
*"Yippee!"*

Yes! Breathe to that!

Become that!

And keep breathing…

# A Few Resources

We are living in times of great transition and new understandings. We are on the cusp of new awakenings individually and collectively about the mind/body connection, and about how meditating in the body can produce dramatic results. Important research is being done that is shifting our understanding of the material plane we thought we knew so well.

These books have been personal favorites, written by modern pioneers who are charting new levels of understanding as well as remembering and documenting what a few great ones have known since the beginning of time: the great healing potential that lives within all of us. Be inspired by them *and* begin to gain your own experiences!

Ahern, Adrianne, Ph.D., ***Back in Charge,*** Boulder, Sentient Press, 2009.

Alcamo, I. Edward, Ph.D, ***Anatomy Coloring Book,*** New York: Random House, 2003.

Borysenko, Joan, Ph.D., ***The Power of the Mind to Heal,*** Hay House, 1995.

Chilton Pearce, Joseph, ***The Biology of Transcendence: A Blueprint of the Human Spirit,*** Rochester, Vermont: Park Street Press, 2002

Church, Dawson, and Sherr, M.D., Alan, ***The Heart of the Healer,*** New York: Aslan, 1987.

Dossey, M.D., Larry, *Healing Words: The Power of Prayer and the Practice of Medicine,* New York: HarperCollins,1993.

Ewing, William A., *Inside Information: Imaging the Human Body,* New York: Simon and Schuster, 1996.

Gaynor, M.D., Mitchell, *Sounds of Healing,* New York: Broadway Books, 1999.

Hawkes, Joyce Whitely, *Cell-Level Healing: The Bridge from Soul to Cell,* New York: Atria Books, 2006

Kabat-Zinn, Jon, *Coming to Our Senses: Healing Ourselves and the World through Mindfulness,* New York: Hyperion, 2005.

Leonard, George, and Murphy, Michael, *The Life We Are Given: A Long-Term Program for Realizing The Potential of Body, Mind, Heart, and Soul,* New York: Putnam Books, 1995.

Lipton, Ph.D., Bruce, *The Biology of Belief: Unleashing the Power of Consciousness, Matter, and Miracles,* Santa Rosa, California: Elite Books, 2005.

Mayer, Ph.D., Elizabeth Lloyd, *Extraordinary Knowing: Science, Skepticism, and the Inexplicable Powers of the Human Mind,* NY: Bantam Books, 2007.

Mehl-Madrona, M.D., Lewis, *Coyote Medicine,* New York: Scribner, 1997.

Moss, M.D., Richard, *The Black Butterfly: An Invitation to Radical Aliveness,* Berkeley: Celestial Arts, 1986.

Murphy, Michael, *The Future of the Body,* NY: Perigee Books, 1992.

Ornish, M.D., Dean, *Love and Survival: The Scientific Basis for the Healing Power of Intimacy,* New York: HarperCollins, 1998.

Ornish, M.D., Dean, *The Spectrum: A Scientifically Proven Program to Feel Better, Live Longer,* New York: Ballantine Books, 2007

Pert, Ph.D., Candace, *Molecues of Emotion: Why You Feel the Way You Feel,* New York: Scribner, 1997.

Roizen, M.D., Michael F., and Oz MD, Mehmet, *You: The Owner's Manual,* NY: Harper and Collins, 2008

Sheldrake, Ph.D., Rupert, *The Science of Life: The Hypothesis of Formative Causation,* Houghton Mifflin, 1981.

Siegel, M.D., Bernie, *Love, Medicine, and Miracles,* New York: Harper and Row, 1986.

Wilber, Ken, *A Brief History of Everything,* Boston: Shambhala, 1996

Institute of Noetic Sciences, *Shift: At the Frontiers of Consciousness,* quarterly journal. These people are at the cutting edge of Mind-Body research!

## Poetry and Quotations:

Adler-Beléndez, Ekiwah, *Weaver,* Amatlán, Morelos, México, Ediciones del Arkan, 2003.

Carson, Anne, *Eros: the Bittersweet,* Dalkey Archive Press, 1998.

Evans, Lynnette (editorial selection), *Wisdom for Life,* New Jersey: Chartwell Books, 2004.

Hirshfield, Jane with Aratani, Mariko, *The Ink Dark Moon, Love Poems by Ono no Komachi and Isumi Shikibu, Women of the Ancient Court of Japan*, NY: Vintage Books, 1986.

Hirshfield, Jane (editor), *Women in Praise of the Sacred: 43 Centuries of Spiritual Poetry by Women*, New York: HarperPerennial, 1994.

Ladinsky, Daniel, *Love Poems from God: Twelve Sacred Voices from the East and West*, New York: Penguin, 2002.

Ladinsky, Daniel, *The Gift: Poems by Hafiz the Great Sufi Master*, New York: Penguin, 1999.

Rumi (translated by John Moyne and Coleman Barks), *Say I Am You*, Athens, GA: Maypop, 1994.

Ryan, MJ (editor), *A Grateful Heart: Daily Blessings for the Evening Meal from Buddha to the Beatles*, Berkeley: Conari Press, 1994.

## Acknowledgments by Barry for:

~ My co-author for her patience, integrity, truth and joy.

~ My wife, Adrianne, who breathes with me.

~ My children and grandchildren who keep me young.

~ Gene Farley, a wonderful Buddhist, in whose presence I experienced transcendence beyond the cell.

~ Dr. Rocco Ruggiero, passionate, always curious and never willing, no matter how old or lame, to learn to tap dance.

~ All my teachers, too many to list.

~ Seth Franklin, a determined patriot, teacher, and quotation collector.

~ All those I've forgotten.

## Acknowledgments by Patricia for:

~ My teacher, Barry, for vast stores of patience, insight and love.

~ Antón, scholar, lover of wisdom and most excellent son.

~ Heather Kibbey, who encouraged us to publish the book and generously made it happen.

~ My patients and students, who teach me, but let me think I'm the teacher.

~ My teacher, Rosa Beléndez, for seeing me.

~ My teacher, Richard Moss, who opened doors of awareness.

~ My partner, Jim, for standing outside the box.

~ All those who have loved me, too numerous to name.

# Index

## A



## B



## C



## D



## E



## F



## G



## H

## I - J



## K



## L



## M



## O - P



## R



## S



## T - U - V



## W

We invite you to visit our website at:

**www.CellLevelMeditation.com**

for more information.

Additional copies of this book,

Cell Level Meditation

Breathing with The Wisdom & Intelligence of the Cell

are available at bookstores, Amazon.com
or directly from Simply Wonder, LLC

We can be reached at: **SimplyWonder@gmail.com**

- to order a book ($12.95, plus applicable tax, and shipping)
- to request a 20% discount on book orders of 10 or more
- to inquire about workshops or speaking engagements
- to share with us your personal experiences with Cell Level Meditation (with your written permission, we're happy to include them on the website)

**Simply Wonder, LLC**
PO Box 12591
Olympia, WA 98508

**website:** www.CellLevelMeditation.com
**email:** SimplyWonder@gmail.com